ENDORSEMENTS FOR WHEN ICE CREAM IS NOT ENOUGH

Everyone from time to time hits bumps on their road of life. Bumps raise negative emotions like annoyance, anxiety, and sadness and can cause tensions between you and others. Ellen Gendelman and Renee Jaspan empathically and engagingly narrate multiple examples. Together these multiple vignettes illustrate how, with or without the help of a therapist, you can learn to convert moments of distress and dissension into opportunities for win-win solutions. Bravo on this heart-opening book. Its stories are sure to help readers face their own challenges with increased insight, compassion and effectiveness.

—Susan Heitler, PhD, author of *Prescriptions Without Pills: For Relief From Depression, Anger, Anxiety and More*, with free worksheets and videos at prescriptionswithoutpills.com

In *When Ice Cream Is Not Enough*, authors Ellen Gendelman and Renee Jaspan explore the dynamics of human relationships through characters who tell interesting stories. They have chosen their tales wisely as they write about family, friend and work relationships utilizing situations which represent the human experience in our present-day society. Each chapter explores some aspect of relationship-parent/child struggles at different life stages, sibling relationships, in/law problems, friend issues, work conflicts and stresses- from the perspective of each of the participants. In so doing, Gendelman and Jaspan illuminate the complexity of interactions. They help the reader recognize that the resolution of problems comes not from judgment and certainty but rather from openness, curiosity and a willingness and ability to recognize and validate one's own feelings as well as those of the other. They provide clear, easily understandable guidelines of ways of expanding one's repertoire of responses to self-regulate emotions to develop mutually satisfying relationships and resolve struggles.

In the final section Gendelman and Livingston are clear about healthy principles of iCare-Internal Compassion and Relationship Enhancement. They guide the reader through step by step questions which increase self-awareness and give specific, useful suggestions for managing difficult feelings which occasionally hijack us and prevent us from functioning at our best. Their wisdom is both easily accessible and yet profound.

—Janice Starkman Goldfein LMSW

Gendelman, and Jaspan have written a practical book that provides clear guidelines on how to use self-examination, and openness to the perspective of others to deepen and enhance our relationships with family member, friends, and colleagues. Scenarios depicting conflicts between family members, and friends or acquaintances allow the reader to manage interpersonal conflict in a manner that can lead to a greater sense of harmony and peace in connection with others. I recommend this book for all who are looking to develop their ability to deepen their relationships in an honest mature and meaningful way.

—David Pelcovitz, Ph.D, Psychologist

The ability to see from another person's perspective is not only the hallmark of mental health, but is at the cornerstone of successful relationships. Highly engaging and richly insightful "When Ice Cream is Not Enough" offers readers ample opportunity to enhance this invaluable ability and to improve the quality of our interactions in both our personal and professional lives.

—David J Lieberman, Ph.D.
Acclaimed Speaker and NYT Bestselling Author

WHEN ICE CREAM IS NOT ENOUGH

STORIES THAT NURTURE LOVING RELATIONSHIPS

Ellen Gendelman
and Renee Jaspan

Copyright © 2017 by Ellen Gendelman and Renee Jaspan.

All rights reserved. No part of this publication may be reproduced, distributed or transmitted in any form or by any means, including photocopying, recording, or other electronic or mechanical methods, without the prior written permission of the publisher, except in the case of brief quotations embodied in critical reviews and certain other noncommercial uses permitted by copyright law. For permission requests, write to the publisher, addressed "Attention: Permissions Coordinator," at the address below.

Ellen Gendelman and Renee Jaspan
26040 Marlowe Pl
Oak Park, Michigan 48237

www.Awindowwithin.net
awindowwithin@gmail.com

Publisher's Note: This is a work of narrative non-fiction. Names, places, and incidents are a product of the author's imagination. Locales and public names are sometimes used for atmospheric purposes. Any resemblance to actual people, living or dead, or to businesses, companies, events, institutions, or locales is completely coincidental.

Adapted from *The Missing Peace* published by Menucha Publisher 2016

Book Layout ©2017 Tracy R Atkins

When Ice Cream is Not Enough / Ellen Gendelman and Renee Jaspan
1st ed.

CS Print Edition ISBN: 978-0-692-83350-6
IS Print Edition ISBN: 978-0-692-92677-2
eBook Edition ISBN: 978-0-692-83351-3

I dedicate this book in loving memory of my dear parents Gil and Judy Ostro both of whom passed away in the prime of their lives.

After my father died, my mother continued to speak about my father lovingly. Despite her shattered dreams of growing old with her husband, she cherished the loving relationship that they had shared over nine years.

The special closeness they shared taught volumes about the importance of secure nurturing relationships. And I hope that they derive special joy as they look down from their special place on High and see their legacy continued.

Acknowledgments

We would like to thank Mrs. Janice Goldfein, Dr. Susan Heitler, Dr. David Lieberman, and Dr. David Pelcovitz for their enthusiastic approbations of our project. You took time from your already demanding schedules to give us encouragement, constructive feedback and blessings. Tracy's expertise shines through every page, along with his patience as we constantly refined and tweaked. I want to thank my dear neighbor and friend Sara Eisemann for her encouragement and gifted pen in helping to frame the design. I also want to express heartfelt appreciation to my dear neighbors and friends Jonathan and Kayla Adlerstein for the fun filled, and thought-provoking brainstorming session which gave birth to this phenomenal title. Davonia kept creating and recreating covers until we felt completely satisfied without one word of complaint. They continued to pitch with positivity. And to our personal editor and proof reader Gabi Drissman, who cheered us on from the first moment and provided valuable editorial corrections and feedback, we express our gratitude.

Ellen's Acknowledgments

How can I begin to acknowledge the many people who shaped my life, influenced me and guided me at every stage of life? Every encounter offers a learning opportunity. Teachers, students, friends, mentors, colleagues, clients, neighbors, acquaintances and even critics all taught me valuable knowledge, enhanced my self-awareness and contributed to my growth. The only possibility is to pay it forward which is one of my goals with this book.

I want to give a special thank you to my dear in laws, Mr. and Mrs. I Gendelman who provide a sterling example of love and commitment for their children. I am one of your fortunate beneficiaries. Even though we live far away, we feel your warmth in close proximity. May G-d bless you with many healthy and happy years together and great pleasure from your children, grandchildren and great grandchildren.

I want to thank my very dear friend Dr. Sharon Livingston who taught me to create a space for play no matter how demanding our schedules might be. You transformed my morning cup of coffee into a cherished routine. Thank you for reading every story, providing valuable feedback and for sharing your expertise as we coauthored the ICARE section of this book together.

Renee, my very dear friend ever since we were young and coauthor...we did it together! Yes, I thought I was the "bossy older sister" in our friendship but who was the task master propelling us forward from the inception of this project until the very last word? I admire your sensitivity, love of giving, patience, and your wonderful contagious laugh that makes our husbands just look at us helplessly until we wipe away the tears and sigh with deep delight. We have shared happiness and pain and only become closer through the years. Thank you for the gift of your children who I adore as if they would be my own nieces and nephews. Thank you for always being there like a loving sister.

My dearest children, Avrohom and Malki, Shimon and Brocha, Azi and Shaindi, Nachi and Sora and Sruli--- Each of you gives us more than you can ever realize. Your optimism, your close connection to one another, your continuous striving for growth ... Raising you from infancy and knowing that our bond only gets deeper fills me with indescribable joy. You truly give hope and inspiration to other parents who came home from teachers' meetings in elementary school needing Tylenol. And watching you as couples building a life together and raising your precious children with love and care gives us endless joy and a few laughs when we see your children behaving in ways that bring back memories. Sruli, we love having you close to home. And, when you are ready to fly from the nest, we know that you together with your siblings will always have a place in our hearts and in our home.

And, Baruch, how do I begin to thank you for over thirty years of marriage? Your devotion to our family and quiet humility create an environment where I feel loved and cherished, appreciated and encouraged. You patiently waited for your eighteen year old bride to grow up and perhaps might still be waiting. There are no words to thank you for being my caring husband and for modeling the gold standard of acceptance and love for our children to emulate.

And finally, I thank G-d for giving me life and the myriad blessings that accompany me every step of the journey.

May G-d continue to bless us together with all of His children.

Contents

Section One: All in the Family 1
I am Floored! 3
    Mom Speaks: 3
    Michelle Speaks: 6
No Pizza For Me?! 10
    Mommy Speaks: 10
    Barbara Speaks: 12
Can it Be? 17
    Nicolle Speaks: 17
    Helene Speaks: 19
Mathmatically Speaking! 23
    Mother Speaks: 23
    Debbie Speaks: 25
What's the Big Deal? 27
    Beverly Speaks: 27
    Steve Speaks: 29
Hurried and Harried 32
    Rebecca Speaks: 32
    Mommy Speaks: 34
Forlorn and Forgotten 36
    Mary's Mother Speaks: 36
    Susie's Mother Speaks: 38
Porcupine Quills 42
    Marla Speaks: 42
    Mom Speaks: 44

- Koalas, Here We Come 47
  - Evie Speaks: 47
  - Mommy Speaks: 50
- Meet Your New Grandson 53
  - Mom Speaks: 53
  - Sally Speaks: 57
- Surprise Package 59
  - Rachel Speaks: 59
  - Eileen Speaks: 62
- Tentacles of Fear 66
  - Shelly Speaks: 66
  - Mom Speaks: 69
- Shattered Dreams 71
  - Ann Speaks: 71
  - Albert Speaks: 73
- Yikes Mom's Moving In! 77
  - Stephanie Speaks: 77
  - Allen Speaks: 79
- Section Two: Allies and Alibies 81
- Fired! 82
  - April Speaks: 82
  - Director Karen Speaks: 84
- Oh Look! 87
  - Karly Speaks: 87
  - Stuey Speaks: 90
- And the Winner Is 93
  - Principal Speaks: 93
  - Mrs. Stamps Speaks: 95
- A Little 'Cell-f' Reflection 97

 Libby Speaks: 97

 Cashier Speaks: 99

Passing the Buck 104

 Betty Speaks: 104

 Rhoda Speaks: 108

A Telling Moment 112

 Karla Speaks: 112

 Ronny Speaks: 114

Bittersweet Chocolate 118

 Denise Speaks: 118

 Mrs. Chocolate Confection Speaks: 120

Triangular Trauma 124

 Peggy Speaks: 124

 Fern Speaks: 126

Those are the Brakes 129

 Mark Speaks: 129

 Scott Speaks: 131

On Call 135

 Nervous Mom Speaks: 135

 Samantha Speaks: 137

The Extra Mile 141

 Tara Speaks: 141

 Becky Speaks: 144

Ruling My Roost 147

 Jill Speaks: 147

 Jasmine Speaks: 151

Book-Nook 154

 Anna Speaks: 154

 Mrs. Mekovsky Speaks: 159

A Work Of Art 162
   Gail Speaks: 162
   The Boss Speaks: 167
A Piece of the Pie 170
   Joy Speaks: 170
   Diane Speaks: 173
Section Three: ICARE 177
ICARE 179
   Assessment: 181
   Interventions from "What's the Big Deal" to help Beverly and Steve understand one another and repair their hurt ...184
   Marla works through her anger with her own inner Self-Counselor 190
   April utilizes the ICARE Model after being fired as she works as her own "self-counselor". 194
   Betty uses the ICARE model to work through her hurt at being criticized for misallocating charity funds. 198
   Karla successfully works through her fear of sharing her illness with Steve using the ICARE model 202
   Dear Readers, ...204
About the Author 206

Section One:
All in the Family

I am Floored!

MOM SPEAKS / MICHELLE SPEAKS

Mom Speaks:

The call from my married daughter started off innocently enough. Why did I think she was just calling to touch base without having a deeper agenda?

"Hi, Michelle, how are you, sweetie?"

She answered with platitudes, and then proceeded to regale me with the latest episodes of the kids' various stages of development. I listened with feigned patience, subduing my yawns and longing to sink into my novel for a few luxurious minutes before falling into bed. But motherhood is based on love and devotion, certainly not offered only when it's convenient.

"So, Mike was diagnosed with a speech and language processing disorder," Michelle continued, and suddenly my fatigue vanished as I listened intently, clutching the phone and feeling my daughter's pain. "And the therapist said that's why he has social issues."

"Oh, Michelle," I breathed, "I'm sorry."

Thinking of the years of struggle we went through with our Sean - he, too, had learning issues and social difficulties- I wondered if Michelle blamed our genes for the problems Mike was having. It's not our fault, though, is it? These things can happen, even if genetics are involved. You know that, right, Michelle?

Anyway, the therapist recommended a great sleep-away camp for Mike. She thought it would be great for him to have a relaxed atmosphere in the summer and to get a new start socially where the kids don't know him and look down on him as a weak student and a kid with problems. And they actually work on social skills in this camp, too. I already spoke to the director."

"Sounds like an amazing opportunity," I said, wishing such a thing had been available when we were dealing with Sean. "What camp is this?"

"It's called Camp Connection. But," she hemmed, "there's a slight problem."

I waited, holding my breath and feeling a fluttery sense of premonition.

"The tuition is $3,000 for one session."

I whistled loudly, my heart plummeting straight to my stomach.

"Do- do you think you and Dad might be able to help us with this?" Michelle asked, and I could picture her bright blue eyes staring straight into mine, pleading.

A laden silence stretched between us as my mind whirled and stirred a confused jumble of thoughts. Three thousand dollars? But that's how much our new kitchen floor costs! I've only waited five years, five long years of watching the holes in the floor grow by the day, grimacing every time I sweep and notice another piece of the wood fraying. And finally Mo and I decided we would put in a new floor this year, and the contractor is actually scheduled to come in this Wednesday with some samples. Would I have to shelve my long awaited dream for my grandson's needs? Is that fair? Don't parents have needs, too?

"Ma?" Michelle intruded on my silent reverie, and I realized I hadn't given her an answer.

"Let me talk with Dad," I said. "Of course we'd love to help. The question is what we're able to do. I'll let you know soon, okay?"

As I hung up and balled my fists in frustration, I watched the dream of my new floor sprout wings and sail through the open window, soaring heavenward. I knew that somehow we would wind up giving the money to Michelle. What doesn't one do for a child and grandchild? They're more important than a mere floor, right? But it's not just a floor, I countered. I'm embarrassed when we have company. And I'm tired of living like this- it's affecting my quality of life. Besides, we had no one to turn to while we were raising our kids to help us with extras like this. We had to do everything on our own. So maybe it's okay to say no. Michelle will understand, won't she? She knows we struggle with money, and we help when we can. But what will she say if I tell her a regretful no, and then she comes over and sees a magnificent new kitchen floor? Something tells me she won't really get it, and then our relationship might be damaged irreparably... Can someone please tell me what to do? You sacrifice your whole life for your kids- does it ever end? Are you ever able to take care of your own needs?

Michelle Speaks:

"Happy anniversary to you, too. Can you believe it's been ten years already?" We sat together with hot cups of cocoa, reminiscing as we celebrated.

"Ten wonderful years. I couldn't have asked for a better wife and mother for our children, Michelle. I probably should tell you that more but somehow in the everyday hectic pace of life, we don't tend to speak this way."

"Thank you, David. Maybe we need to call and thank our friend for introducing us again." These positive thoughts brought my mind to my greatest insecurity, my son. "But, David—about being a wonderful mother—I just don't feel that any of the methods that I have used successfully with our other children work effectively with Mike. It's almost as if he doesn't hear me or doesn't want to hear me. I get so scared when his behavior seems so out of control. I just can't help wondering what the future holds for him. He reminds me of..."

David gave me a knowing look and said, "Michelle, don't torment yourself. Listen to me. You're a fantastic mother. You take parenting classes. You ask advice from experienced mothers. You work on yourself not to respond reactively, but in ways that are conducive to our children's learning. And, what about all the various therapy appointments that you expended time and resources on for the last couple of years? Knowing both of our parents' tight finances, we tightened our belts and paid out of our own pockets. You gave up fancy jewelry to polish your living diamonds. And, you must admit that Mike's tantrums have decreased."

"David, you're a phenomenal defense attorney to my harsh inner critic. I know you're right, but I worry that he is suffering and doesn't fit in socially with his classmates. His learning challenges affect his self-esteem and sometimes he just looks up at me with this confused look on his face as though he really doesn't understand what the world is asking of him."

"Michelle, your intuition is usually on the mark. How about if we enjoy our anniversary dinner and make an appointment with the school tomorrow to glean as much information as possible? Maybe there's another helpful tool that we haven't yet encountered." He stood up and headed toward the counter, "May I please taste a piece of that delicious looking cream cake that you somehow managed to find time to bake?" After I nodded, he cut two generous slices, a delicious treat for such a special milestone. As I ate the first bite, I resolved to contact the principal and see if he could help.

•••

I came home no more than a week later replaying the scene in my mind. David and I sat around a mahogany table together with the principal to see if he had any new suggestions.

"Mr. and Mrs. Stern, thank you for your trust in our school and for your active cooperation. We believe that partnership between parents and teachers holds the key to student success. Although Mike has made significant progress academically and behaviorally, his recent comprehensive testing revealed a speech and language processing disorder. We will notify the teachers so that we can individualize Mike's learning goals and provide two hours of remedial services each day.

"There is another idea that may be very helpful as well. A new camp opened which uses research-based methods to help children with challenges similar to Mike's. They have an excellent success rate. The only drawback is that it is quite expensive. Since they have a very low therapist-student ratio, at this point, there are no reductions available. May I suggest that you discuss this at home and contact me if you would like me to write a personal recommendation for Mike? I truly think this would be an ideal fit for him and that he would thrive in their stimulating environment."

I leaned back in the chair thinking hard. David was doing the same.

"David, are you thinking what I am thinking?"

Defensive, he spoke up, misunderstanding me, "Michelle, my father has been unemployed for years now."

"David, I know, I was thinking of my parents. It's so hard to ask. My parents never even sent us to camp because there was never enough money to afford that luxury for so many children. And frequently that was the response our parents gave us. We were always allowed to earn our own money, but anything beyond food, shelter and some clothing was considered a luxury. I still remember feeling resentful when all of my friends went to camps and ate regularly in restaurants. It seems almost ludicrous, or maybe satisfying on some primitive level, to ask them to sponsor their grandson's camp. Yet, money continues to be so tight for them. Covering the mortgage, high insurance costs, hosting us all during the holiday season...

"Now that we have to pay bills, I understand so much better, although the little girl in me still wants Mom to come to the rescue. It is their grandchild.

"Lately Mom has mentioned wanting to fix up their house. None of us appreciate staying there, as it is looking more and more run-down. Yet we all keep asking for help. If we can't go to our parents when we have needs, then who *can* we approach?

"David, how can I feel entitled to ask while guilty at the same time? I'm so confused. Wouldn't Mom and Dad want Mike to have this opportunity? Aren't we the most important people in their lives? Isn't it normal to approach parents when we have needs? We would want our children to always feel free to ask us!

"Okay, are you calling or am I calling? If this is the right thing to do, explain the shaky hands, sweaty palms and pounding heart!"

I picked up the phone and dialed their number, nervousness bubbling inside of me. When she answered I was barely able to speak. "Hello, Mom, How are you, it's Michelle speaking..." Umm...So... Like... And...Yeah...

No Pizza For Me?!

MOMMY SPEAKS / BARBARA SPEAKS

Mommy Speaks:

"Hi, Barbara! How was your day?"

I turned from my pots the day before Thanksgiving to give Barbara a smile as she walked into the kitchen. Picking up an empty pizza box, she looked at me questioningly.

"Is there pizza?" she wanted to know, her eyes looking hopeful.

"Afraid not, sweetie," I answered. "Nathan and Libby had some, and there's no more."

"How could you do that?" Barbara's voice was strident. "You know I love pizza! How could you get it and not save some for me?"

Breathless from extensive preparations since all of our out-of-town children and grandchildren were visiting, I didn't really feel up to being my daughter's punching bag at the moment. Maybe another time. I was working so hard to make everyone comfortable with their food and lodgings, and now... I sighed.

"It's a short afternoon, Barb. And I made you a lunch this morning. We got exactly enough for the people who needed to eat. I didn't think you needed two lunches."

"It's not fair! You always give them the best things just 'cuz they don't live at home anymore. I don't count at all. Oh, no. Give me noodles and that's fine. But when they come in, they get pizza."

I furrowed my eyebrows, unsure where this onslaught was coming from. Hadn't I just taken her out yesterday for a special ice cream date before all the kids came in? Was it ever enough, or would I always be found lacking?

"Why didn't you get me some?" she demanded, hands on her hips and eyes flashing furiously. "You never think of me."

Immediately my mental Rolodex rewound to our ice cream trip from yesterday, and then continued to play images of the countless things I've done for this child since she first appeared in this world.

"What do you mean?" I countered, moving over to slice tomatoes for the salad. "I made you pancakes the other day, drove you to play practice, got you ice cream...what exactly do you mean that I never think of you?"

"They're just more important since they're married and don't live at home," she snarled, placing special emphasis on the word married. "I don't count. I'm a nothing. And besides, our family is so embarrassing. I am the only one in my entire school with married siblings and an annoying little sister at home."

Clamping my lips shut so I wouldn't say anything I'd regret, I withdrew into a subdued silence, praying that G-d should take the wind out of her sails. Tired and overworked, I really didn't feel up to a full-fledged teenage uprising at the moment. But it just wasn't fair, I rued, dicing the green peppers and throwing them into the large salad bowl. Just when I'm working my hardest and trying my best to do everything for everyone, why is that the time to take aim and fire at Mommy for failing once again?

Barbara Speaks:

In a way, although I would not tell Mommy, (because I'd rather that she pick me up most of the time), the walk home from school is positive. It gives me a chance to air my thoughts. In some ways, I just love when my married siblings come to visit. The house is so lively and exciting and the table-talk so interesting. My brothers-in-law are fun, and I wouldn't admit to anyone that I actually enjoy when they tease me. And the babies are adorable, even though I need to fight with my eight-year-old sister for holding rights- absolutely ridiculous, if you ask me. But, now we are getting to the crux of the problem, which is – NO ONE DOES ASK ME!

When my married siblings are away, it's a chorus of "Barbara do this, and oh, Barb, can you just...?"

When they come home, it's as if I become a second-class citizen. They have no responsibilities and are treated like royal visitors. Yours truly has much more work as a result, yet only gets to eat their leftover scraps.

It really hurts. Mommy knows that pizza is my absolute favorite food in the whole world. What does having already eaten lunch have to do with pizza anyway? Sometimes the logic of parents is utterly befuddling.

I wish Mommy would understand that when they come and she expects so much more from me that I need more privileges instead of feeling like I am back to being one of the little ones practically being given a bed time again. Can you imagine the indignity of an eighth grader being sent to bed, and in front of her brothers-in-law, no less?

Maybe I should speak to someone about this. Wonder if anyone else ever felt like this? On the one hand, part of me feels bad for Mommy. She wants to make a nice visit for her children and misses them when they are away, yet she works so hard the whole time they are here, she hardly gets to see them. Somehow, I feel like a prop, designed to help make this picture perfect visit. But I do wonder what is it about marriage that seems to take helpful, capable girls and turn them into couch potatoes when they visit their parents.

Hey, I just had an idea –maybe I should find a nice guy, and then I can also sit and visit while my eight-year-old sister does all the work. Oh, what a totally lovely picture. I want to blow that up in my mind. She is so spoiled. Mommy hardly asks her to do anything, and she cannot do any wrong.

Seriously, my parents seem to misconstrue anything I say as rude or inappropriate, so even when I start out trying to just express my point of view, I get cut off, which makes me really angry. They just tell me to be grateful for all of my privileges and appreciate how few responsibilities I really have compared to when they were children. Isn't it a nuisance when parents do that? I know my mother had to clean half the house weekly because her mother was a widow and worked to support the family, and her sister was never much help in the cleaning department. Maybe I take after that aunt of mine although now she seems to actually enjoy helping Mommy in the kitchen, even (gasp!) washing the dishes. Other than that flaw, she is a lot of fun and seems to get my way of thinking. She also never understood why I need to choke down food that I do not like because children are starving in Africa. And she thinks I am very funny! On the other hand, she's also a therapist- imagine the stigma if anyone found out! But maybe I'm being silly. After all, I know my secrets are safe with her. And above all, she's my aunt, not my therapist.

Maybe I'll go to her for help with this situation. I do love my siblings and enjoy seeing them. But everything is so complicated. If only we could get a live-in maid to do all the work so we can just sit around and talk. And maybe that little eight-year-old sister of mine can go sleep at a friend's house for a couple of days.

•••

It was a great idea to talk to my aunt who did not seem shocked at my outburst and really seemed to accept my feelings.

At first, I felt a bit funny picturing how "nerdy" it seemed to actually speak to a therapist. But, then I told myself this is my aunt and maybe she can really help me, and what my friends don't know won't hurt them, or me, for that matter. My aunt listened carefully, and I could tell that she understood. It was a relief to express my feelings without having to worry that I might hurt someone by doing so and then wallow in the guilt afterwards, which is the absolute worst feeling in the world!

My aunt knows how much I love acting and asked if I wanted to do some role-playing with her. That actually sounded like fun, so I agreed. Besides, it's nice to have someone ask me what I want for a change. It beats being Barbara the prop.

She asked if she could be me and I could play my mother- now this was getting both interesting and a bit frightening at the same time. I agreed again, although a bit more tentatively this time. What did this unpredictable lady have up her sleeve?

I heard her speaking about hypnosis to my mother- you don't think she could hypnotize me without my knowledge, do you? Come on Barb, you trust her, remember? And you asked to speak with her, so get over it and stop behaving like a baby, especially if you don't want everyone else to treat you like one. Okay, boy she actually sounds like me. Listen to this:

"Mommy, I see you got pizza today. Do you mind if I ask you a favor? I really love pizza and it's hard to come home from a tough day at school just to see the empty crumbs sitting in the box. Would you mind keeping me in mind next time this happens, even if I already had a meal? You know, I am never too full for a yummy slice of my favorite food. Thanks, Mommy."

How do I think my mother would react? Probably a lot differently than the way I approached her the first time. Hmmm, that was just the first part of our conversation and then we went on to discuss older sisters getting married and how it affects the single ones at home. She really gave me food for thought and as long as my friends were nowhere in the vicinity (I scanned the area first), I actually gave her a hug. She looked pleasantly surprised. She also looked thrilled at my conclusions at the end of our chat.

Although for some reason, this situation with my married siblings makes me see red, and I do lash out at my mother in a way that makes me feel like a worm afterwards. I am really going to try to enjoy all the good parts of this visit. And my sisters are really a lot of fun- maybe, just maybe, they want to enjoy a break when they visit since it's a vacation for them from their regular load of housework and childcare.

Could that be what's going on here? Can I possibly be misinterpreting Mommy's desire to give them a break as not caring about my needs?

Maybe I need to take a walk more often- hey, how about a walk to the pizza shop!

Now that's an idea, and I will give my aunt the olives because she seems to be on another one of her endless new diets, although she does not let me use that word- she calls it a "lifestyle change."

Hmmm- a life style change- can I really work on communicating to my parents without sarcasm so they can focus on my feelings? Maybe I should ask about hypnotizing my tongue.

Fortified with pizza, minus the olives, I feel energized and ready to try again.

Can it Be?

NICOLLE SPEAKS / HELENE SPEAKS

Nicolle Speaks:

Can it be? Will I really hold a new gift of life in nine months' time, another precious miracle that G-d has gifted us?

Oh, but then I think of my sister...the stain on my happiness that sends my joy plummeting into a nosedive. My dear and only sister, Helene, has been married several years longer than I, and has still not been blessed with children, while I, her younger sister, am going on to have my third. She has struggled with infertility over the years, tried numerous interventions that have taxed her both physically and emotionally. How will I tell her my news and cause her more pain? Maybe I won't share the news yet- it's still early.

I sometimes wish I could give her some of my fertility as a gift. Why, I wonder, does pregnancy come to me so easily that I don't have time to wonder and worry, while for her, there is endless waiting, accompanied by the fear that she might never have someone to call her Mommy?

She probably thinks I'm oblivious to her pain, living in my own little bubble of baby-happiness, while in truth, I drink from her bitter cup in large doses, almost as if it's happening to me. We're so close, and it's agonizing to watch her suffer. She and her husband are so good, so fine, deserve life's blessings… All I know is that it hurts me too, more than she will ever know. Because when you love someone, it hurts to see them in pain.

Just the other day, Helene came over to visit. She invited us to go out to the mall; they have a fun play area that she knows my kids love. "Sure," I agreed. But then I had to nurse the baby, and I could see her fidgeting. When I thought we were finally ready to go, the baby spit up, and I had to change both of our outfits- his and mine. Then my toddler had a dirty diaper… "You know what?" Helene finally suggested, heading for the door. "I'll just meet you there."

"Okay," I agreed, while feeling almost guilty for being so consumed with my babies. It's not my fault! I wanted to say. But I winced as I glimpsed the pain in her eyes. Then a few nights later it happened again. Helene called me and needed a recipe. The baby picked that moment to start screaming, so I couldn't talk. "Can I call you later when things quiet down?" I asked. "Sure," she agreed, but I heard the silence coming from her end of the line, and I sighed. Her home was so painfully quiet. She had finished her work, cleaned up supper from two, and was free to pursue other venues. But I knew her secret wish: if only she would love to be so busy that she didn't have time to make a simple phone call.

Who's calling? Gulp- it's Helene. I hope she won't hear anything in my voice that will give away my secret.

"Hi, Helene how are you? You're just coming from the doctor? Oh, I hope the new treatment works. I know that Marsha had something similar and it was successful. What? That must have been so awkward. It's the worst when people try to avoid you. Did she even say hi? Or pretend you weren't there?

Aha, I guess you are right that it doesn't make it easier. It's obvious why **they** are there. She probably doesn't know what to say to you, it's good that sometimes they try small talk. That must have been uncomfortable for you. And Helene, I continued, my heart hammering violently, "I have something to share with you…"

Helene Speaks:

Dr. Twersky suggested that I use a journal to express my feelings. There is something about writing that allows feelings to surface, even sentiments beneath our conscious level of awareness. Accordingly, I will try to be honest and open for the sake of identifying my feelings to work with them.

One of my characteristics is striving to do and be my very best. In school, any grade lower than an A+, except maybe in math, was akin to failing. If I hurt someone's feelings, that was nothing less than horrific. And, of course, I was not allowed to feel angry or insulted because that was not practicing positive character traits and therefore not in keeping with the person I strived to become. The only problem with all of this boils down to being human. And, so by denying or suppressing any negative feelings, I was just holding them where they theoretically could not come out to bite anyone and dispel my distorted self-image of angelic behavior.

When I married, my husband was still in medical school. I would generously allow him to study to his heart's content, disturbing him only minimally, even when I wanted to spend time with him. And when most of my friends (and my sister) were blessed with children on a yearly basis, I maintained a sparkling clean apartment that remained oh, so quiet, and I felt less worthy and undeserving of being a mother. How could I improve? Clearly, I determined that my jealousy was bad karma. Could I ignore the pain? Growing up with just one sibling, I yearned to be the mother of a warm and lively family.

I cried, prayed, worked on doing more acts of kindness, and tried very hard to rejoice and participate in people's celebrations. Often my efforts bore fruit, and at other moments, they felt futile. When I would visit neighbors, all of their attention was geared to the babies, their feeding and sleeping habits and their adorable antics. What could I contribute without sounding pitiful?

The most intense pain involved my younger sister, Nicolle. Watching her cuddle her adorable infants and stammer and stutter, trying not to cause me pain before she put on maternity clothing yet again, felt excruciating. I knew my response was illogical. She did not contrive this plan. Yet- I was the older sister. Throughout our childhood, I protected her and on some levels felt like a quasi-parent in my father's absence and my mother's lack of formal education. Nicolle was shy and reserved and I paved the way, which she followed appreciatively. But now the tide has changed. How could I relate to her without embarrassment once she became the mother of so many children? Now that she possessed skills and experiences that I didn't, how could she consult me for my opinion? What did I know about juggling two babies two years in a row, valiantly attempting to care for both of their needs? Is it possible that Nicolle would have liked to ask for my guidance but because she perceives my agony, she does not dare? If I exuded serenity, maybe she would once again take counsel and value my sisterly perspective.

Yes, my head knew that G-d gives each of us what we are supposed to have to best fulfill our purpose on this earth. Yet my heart was still protesting at the perceived unfair distribution of blessing.

I coped by overachieving and preparing for my students till the wee hours of the night. I coped by pouring time and energy into community volunteer work, not allowing myself the luxury of relaxation after a long day. I coped by trying to feel worthy. Slowly, I began to grow up and allowed my heart to absorb the truth that my brain understood. Tears still came readily each time my hopes were disappointed- yet the other part of me yearned to find meaning in the blessings that I received and not always pine for that which I didn't have. I have an amazing husband and am blessed with a wonderful marriage. I have a meaningful job that makes me feel fulfilled. Clearly, I could choose to utilize this challenge to grow and abandon this constant comparison that sucked the joy out of every opportunity for gratitude. And, a small voice whispered, do I think that those on the other side of the fence do not have challenges? Be honest, I told myself, every situation contains some pain and you have seen some with your own eyes. Do I choose to continue to live life with the mentality that the grass is always greener on the other side and have that chorus echoing in my thoughts and stealing my enjoyment of each moment?

Life is not a race of how many babies one can produce in the shortest time with the winner having the most children. Life is a truly an individualized contest of trying to be better each day in a real way. The fountains of love that I feel for my sister and her children, who have become cherished nieces and nephews, are the source of great joy that we share. And once I came to that realization, I gave myself permission to love my life exactly the way it is. And when women came crying to me with similar stories of anguish, they felt comforted by my experience, and we gave strength to each other. Then, I knew that my head and my heart were one. Maybe that was G-d's plan all along.

Mathematically Speaking!

MOTHER SPEAKS / DEBBIE SPEAKS

Mother Speaks:

The conversation started off innocently enough. Had I known how it would escalate, I would have put on a suit of armor. Kids these days- you can't win. Debbie came home from school, and we were sitting at the kitchen table eating together.

"So I wanted you to ask Mrs. Leiberman to switch me to the lower math class," Debbie told me, spearing her potato and looking me in the eye.

"Oh," I said, somewhat surprised. "Why?"

"Because I can't do it!" Debbie's eyes flashed with anger and frustration. "I don't belong there."

Looking at my straight A student of a daughter, I felt sure that she was capable of doing the work. Maybe pre-algebra didn't come as easily to her as other subjects, but with a little more effort, I had full confidence in her abilities to succeed. Flashbacks of my trying to help her here and there streamed through my mind, and I knew that my assistance was ineffective- algebra was definitely not my thing. But I had just attended parent teacher conferences. Her math teacher assured me that she was available to help students who were struggling, and that she generously set aside several times a week when students could work with her. She also told me Debbie had improved since the beginning of the year- she had a B average.

"Debbie," I said, "Have you approached your teacher so she can help you? She said she has time."

"I don't want to do that!" Debbie exploded. "I just want to switch to the other class! Why can't you ever help me?"

Okay, Rachel, deep breath. She's just a teenager and doesn't mean to fling mud in your face. At least, I don't think she does.

"But how can I speak to Mrs. Leiberman before you put in some effort? The first thing she's going to ask me is if you got help."

"Mommy." Debbie fixed me with an icy glare. "I can't do the work. I don't understand it and that's it."

"Sweetie," I replied. "I think you're very capable and you can do it- you just have to try. Going to the lower class is a cop out. Who said everything in life is easy? First try, go to the teacher, spend time and-"

"I didn't ask you what you think I should do. I asked you to speak to my principal and get me out of this class!" Debbie shouted. "You know what?" She pushed her chair back and stood up. "I should have known you wouldn't be on my side. Never mind. I'll just go to Mrs. Leiberman myself. I don't know why I thought I could talk to you. Like *you* would understand."

Tossing her ponytail over her shoulder, Debbie flounced out. I heard the door to her room slam closed. Lifting a fork to my mouth, I noticed that my sautéed vegetables were suddenly tasteless. Where had I gone wrong in this conversation? I hadn't empathized- oops! I guess that should have been step one. Maybe I should have tried problem solving together with her? But she didn't really want to problem solve- she wanted me to go along with her pre-decided plan, and I didn't agree with it. Oh, well, I sighed. Maybe next time will go better.

Debbie Speaks:

Waves of anger wash over me. Mothers can be *so* frustrating. And, yes, though I don't like to admit it to myself, much less to her, I do feel guilty. I know it is important to speak respectfully to my parents, but in the school of real life, she just pushes my buttons and I explode.

Sometimes, I do not feel that anyone understands what I go through. And, I guess that makes me feel sad. When I was a little girl, I remember snuggling next to my mother when I felt sad, and she'd hold me and just seem to understand my needs without my saying a word. Now, even when I say many words, it just feels like there is a huge wall between us, and we are speaking two different languages.

Aren't mothers supposed to understand their children? She always says that she knows me better than I know myself. So, then she would know that ever since first grade I am known to my classmates as an A student. Getting a B would lower my status and I'd be teased mercilessly because my classmates know that I push myself to get on honor roll every marking period. For her, a B may mean an improvement. For me it feels like a failure- a failure to achieve the A that is expected of me, and that I expect of myself.

Secondly, my two older siblings went to Ivy League Universities. How will it look if I have to apply to a less academic institution just because of this awful algebra? What's wrong with plain English anyway? Who designed this ridiculous language with X's and Y's that are supposed to balance the world with equality? The only thing it will rebalance is my prized 4.0 GPA!

Mommy always said that everyone has her own talents. I cannot sing, cannot dance, cannot act, cannot get into the really popular group in school. All I have is my straight A average. That's all that makes me special, and I just cannot afford to lose that. And, when I finally plucked up the nerve to reach out to Mommy for help to let me escape this humiliation, she just wants me to keep trying. I feel dumb with this teacher, and it's just too painful to sit there for even one more day.

Sometimes I think that it is not about my feelings. Maybe Daddy and Mommy are embarrassed to have a child in the slower class. They are both prominent people in the community. Yes, that must be it; I am just an embarrassment to them.

Does Mommy remember what it is like to be thirteen?

What's the Big Deal?

BEVERLY SPEAKS / STEVE SPEAKS

Beverly Speaks:

"Have you seen the newest diet?" Mindy, my neighbor, greeted me with a wide smile in the supermarket, pointing to the row of neatly stacked diet shakes and snacks. Was it my imagination, or was she looking over the snacks in my cart with a superior shake of her head? "It's amazing, guaranteed to show results in just twenty-one days or your money back," she continued, seeming oblivious to my reddening face. I watched her place the products in her cart, and then she looked back at me with questioning eyes, wondering if I would follow suit.

My blood rose to a rapid boil as I internalized her not very subtle hint. Yes, I had put on thirty pounds in a relatively short span of time. Stress can do that to people. How dare she assume that I was unaware of what was going on with my own body, and that she had all the answers while I was enveloped by the darkness of ignorance? Just because I had more flab didn't mean a lack of brain cells. Who knew? Maybe my mind had gained weight in the process, too; that could account for some of those pounds, hm?

"Thanks for letting me know," I replied coolly, purposely bypassing the display and moving forward to continue my shopping in a different aisle.

"Can you believe what she said to me?" I fumed aloud later, pouring my wounded feelings into Steve's listening ears. "How rude can she be?!"

Steve cocked his head and shrugged his shoulders. "What's the big deal?" he said. "Why do you have to let her comments get to you?"

Blinking back stinging tears, I turned away so Steve wouldn't see my devastation at his callous response. Who else can you turn to for affirmation and comfort if not to your husband? I needed empathy and reassurance that I was still beautiful, no matter what size I wore. Yet Steve had totally missed the ball, and I was left standing alone in the outfield, watching while the ball flew way out of bounds, a definite foul.

Come to think of it, I rued, furiously attacking a pile of dirty dishes with hot sudsy water, that's his mantra, so why am I surprised? He's often insensitive to my needs for emotional support, and instead of commiserating with me or validating my pain, he'll blithely toss out his, "What's the big deal?" comment and expect me to snap out of my rut. Ramming a clean glass down into the drainer, I was startled when it cracked, leaving sparkling shards all over the counter. Great. Just great. I'd better clean it up before someone gets hurt and it really becomes a big deal.

Sometimes I ask Steve to get me a specific item from the store, which is on his way home from work, and he comes home without it.

"It wasn't on sale today," he explains, tossing bags of all sorts of groceries onto the floor that I didn't need for this week's menu.

How often have I asked him to leave my night table clear of his things so I can have my own little space beside my bed? As it is, we have a small room in a small house, and I don't have adequate space to call my own. All I want is a little corner where I know I can reach for my keys, book, and glasses without having to sift through his junk. Yet time after time, when I bring this matter to his attention, I'm accused of making a big deal out of nothing. And time after time, I find his ties, keys, glasses, or receipts tossed on top of the night table, and have to sift until I find my belongings.

I've tried bringing it to his attention in a calm, gentle manner. I've tried not greeting him with the request, making sure to serve him a nice supper first and ask him about his day. Nothing works. "Just let it go," he tells me, and I simmer in silence.

Should I let it go? Will he never change? How exorbitant is the price for marital harmony? Does it mean always giving in on every issue? But then I feel stepped on and uncared for and wonder- don't my needs matter? Yes, each thing by itself may seem small. But if you take enough small things, they can fill a large space. And as the years have gone by, there is a large space in my heart consumed with anger and resentment and loneliness.

Maybe I'll try that diet after all. As long as Mindy's nowhere around. After all, what's the big deal?

Steve Speaks:

Sometimes I wonder if men and women studied language in different schools and learned different meanings for the same words. My wife, an otherwise intelligent woman relays an incident to me that clearly disturbs her. Like any caring husband, I immediately drop everything else and give her my undivided attention. No multi-tasking or partial attention taking place here. She is clearly hurt by some comment expressed by a less than tactful friend. So, I go the time honored way of any good spouse, and attempt to fix the situation. Isn't that why she shares the event with her loyal and capable husband?

Yet, she then turns to me with anger and disdain as though I did not understand the incident. So, I patiently explain again that the best solution is to forget about it. It's no big deal.

I would not tell her this and certainly would not risk her reading this- but her disdain hurts me. I work hard taking care of the family, giving her time and attention, aim to fix all of her problems. And, on any given day, all I receive lately is a litany of complaints.

I spend time shopping for her, but she mentions the groceries I did not purchase. I shut off my phone and give her attention; she uses this time to complain about my lack of attention to the children. No matter what I do, it just feels that I cannot get it right with her. I put on this strong, masculine front, yet inside I feel so inadequate. I withdraw into my study to protect our connection that I see withering away before my eyes.

At work, when I put on my confident voice, I receive respect. People ask me questions and appreciate the definitive response, which takes a weight off of their shoulders. My style seems to work well at my job and my strengths are appreciated. Yet, every man knows that in the absence of feeling respect from his wife, that show of confidence is merely a façade -an empty shell.

I do not know what to say to her any more that will be appreciated. When her friend hinted to her that a diet might be a good idea, I simply avoided the weight issue. How could I risk even telling her that our affection goes beyond physical appearance? Any time I have tried a comment of that nature, she has simply grabbed a tissue and looked at me with teary eyes clearly waiting for something, but no one told me my lines. That whole topic seems to be sensitive and off limits. The truth is that my wife looks lovely to me- but I do not feel safe saying my true thoughts.

Could I even dare telling her how it feels to walk on eggshells, never knowing if my words are what she expects or needs? It feels way too risky to even try sharing my vulnerable side with her. Perhaps, in addition to the other flaws she already perceives, that would just make her see me as weak and less of a man.

So, where does this leave us but trapped in a pattern of two people who clearly need emotional closeness yet continue to miss the opportunity of providing that safe haven?

Is there anyone who can teach us a common language so that we can be there for one another, which is what we both really want?

Hurried and Harried

REBECCA SPEAKS / MOMMY SPEAKS

Rebecca Speaks:

"Hi, Mom!" I breezed, trundling into my in-laws' home to prepare for my brother's wedding that evening. Breathless and tired after our long car ride, my husband and I herded the kids inside, enjoyed my mother-in-law's delicious and thoughtfully prepared snack, and ran upstairs to get ready.

"Johnny, here's your tie!" I called, trying desperately to fix the tie that he insisted on unclipping every time I got it straight. *Whose idea was it that a three-year-old should wear a tie, anyway? I'd like a word with them.*

"Shelly!" I smiled and held up a gown for my one-year-old toddler. She took one look at me and tore off in the opposite direction, exploding with a loud giggle. I moaned and went in for the chase. Normally I would find this amusing, but since the clock was ticking, it was somewhat nerve wracking. *How much time do we have anyway?* I wondered, looking at my watch for the tenth time in as many minutes.

"Aha! Caught you!" I gave an exuberant victory cry, but Shelly would not be defeated. Tilting her head away from me, she swung her arms with abandon, while I tried vainly to pull the gown over her flailing, protesting body.

Oh, my hair appointment! I touched my towel-covered head and gasped. *I'm supposed to be at the hairdresser in ten minutes. Breathe, Rebecca, breathe.*

Shoving our squalling three-month-old into my bewildered husband's arms, I grabbed the car keys and zoomed off to my appointment. Desperately urging the car through the winding streets of the neighborhood, I gritted my teeth when traffic slowed my journey. *Barry's getting married tonight. Little Barry*...my heart swelled with memories, fond memories of growing up with my terrific younger brother, when suddenly- BEEP! I slammed on the brakes and decided I'd better focus on the road. *Best to leave thinking for later.*

At last we were ready, picture perfect, and in a dazzling, flashing dream, my little brother Barry, became a husband. We ate, we danced, the wedding was magnificent- and then it was over. Piling back in the car, we returned to my in-laws' and collapsed on the couch. My mother-in-law was waiting for us, looking like she wanted to spend some time with us and hear every detail about the wedding and our favorite highlights. *That makes sense*, I thought, *but not now. Not after a day like today. After all, marrying off a little brother is a lot of work*! Physically and emotionally drained, I wanted nothing more than to spend a few quiet minutes talking with my husband before dissolving into a welcome sleep.

"Good night, Ma," I said, pecking her on the cheek and starting up the stairs, beckoning my husband to follow. And I wondered- *is that a tear running down Mommy's cheek? I wonder what happened...*

Mommy Speaks:

Okay, Esther slow down and make a list... Greek yogurt for Rebecca, kiddy yogurt for the baby, how about all of my dear son's favorites-fried chicken, apple pie...

Esther, stop it- it's not Thanksgiving, and they will be so busy running around for this wedding- a varied assortment of filling snacks will add just the right touch.

I am so excited to see them- I must call Sharon and tell her. She is such a wonderful friend and so sensible, too.

"Hi Sharon, You will not believe who is coming to visit. They are coming at a time when we can just sit and talk for hours. Oh, the sheer bliss just to imagine it! I am dancing in the kitchen- good exercise right?

"Why are you telling me to calm down and have realistic expectations? Of all people, I thought you, my friend would be so happy for me. Okay, I guess no one is perfect. I am going to hang up now to prepare the house perfectly and hook up the Netflix in their bedroom."

Maybe, I should stock up on toiletries as it's so easy to forget important items when packing out with young children. Next item on the to-do list: cancelling all of my appointments for three days. After all, what's a bit of money compared to the delightful company of my children?

"Here they come. Come in, so wonderful to see you. Have a delicious bite to eat and then I am here at your service, ready to help you with anything you need."

"Mom, don't you have clients now?"

"Don't worry, I cancelled them to spend quality time together. How often do I get the privilege of seeing you? Fully available and at your service- just say the word.

"Oh, of course I understand that you have so much to do helping your brother with all of his last-minute errands and jitters. I will be just fine here by myself."

I do not usually drink caffeinated coffee at this hour, but I want to be wide-awake for this long awaited talk. It is so important to be there for your children as a listening, non-judgmental ear so they can share their full range of emotions.

"Hello, welcome home, you look like glowing newlyweds your selves. Yes, of course I am still awake and just counting the moments until you returned.

"I have no doubts that it was a beautiful wedding. Come, sit down, and let's hear all about it."

They exchanged a quick glance between them. It appeared that they were way too drained to sit down and review the highlights with me. I valiantly attempted to cover the disappointment that must have been written all over my face. The fact that I had been longing for this moment did not diminish the difficulty of the task. I took a cleansing breath and turned to my children.

"Yes, yes, you need to be well rested before you drive back in the morning. We'll talk another time. Oh, of course I understand- sleep well.

Forlorn and Forgotten

MARY'S MOTHER SPEAKS /
SUSIE'S MOTHER SPEAKS

Mary's Mother Speaks:

"Mommy, can you check your email?" Mary asked the second she came home from school one Thursday afternoon.

The glint in Mary's eye impelled me to stop dicing and chopping, even though I was already running late with dinner preparations. What's a few more minutes? I shrugged, taking a quick detour to my computer.

"No, honey, sorry. There's nothing special there."

"Are you sure?" Mary's eyes looked puzzled. "Ellen, Sandy, and Kathy all said their mothers got emails about Susie's birthday party. It's on Sunday."

"I'm sorry, sweetie," I said. "Maybe it will still come. Or maybe she doesn't have my email address."

Mary shrugged and went back to eating her snack. But I could see that her thoughts were focused on the party.

This scenario repeated itself the moment dinner was finished on Saturday, and several times on Sunday morning. But at this point there was more than confusion reflected in Mary's eyes. There were hurt feelings and glittering tears.

"I'm bored," Mary complained at lunchtime. "And there's no one to play with, because," and here she paused and sniffed, "all of my friends are at the party."

I quietly walked towards the phone and picked it up. *I'll just go to my bedroom and make a quick call,* I thought. *After all, Mary is only eight. I'm sure Susie's mother won't mind having one more child if she knows how much it means to Mary.*

"Mommy, what are you doing?" Mary's eyes narrowed suspiciously. "Are you calling Susie's mother?"

"Uh, I was thinking about it," I admitted, feeling like I had been caught with my hand in the cookie jar.

"Don't," Mary commanded. I reluctantly put the phone down, but I got the message. Yes, she wished she could go to the party, but she wanted to be, well, wanted.

"This is really hard." I kissed the top of her downturned head and put my hand on her shoulder. "You feel left out." Mary lifted watery eyes and gazed into mine, revealing a broken heart.

"I thought she was my friend," she said.

"I know." I paused, my presence and demeanor exuding empathy. "I still wonder if they didn't have my email address. Or here's another possibility. Maybe her mother told her she could only invite a few girls and have a small party."

The afternoon wore on, and Mary's ready smile and carefree attitude remained shadowed. She agreed to come with my husband and me for a walk in the duck pond. We brought her scooter and our leftover bread. But even the swarms of ducks enjoying the feast she threw failed to keep a smile on her face. She scooted along the trail, her lips set in a determined frown, her eyes shuttered. And I watched her, wishing I could wipe away her pain.

By late afternoon, Mary found a friend to play with, and her mood picked up. But the tears were back when I tucked her in that night.

"I'm so sorry," I murmured, giving her a good, long hug. "You're still upset about this, aren't you?" She cried in our embrace, and I lay down next to her until she fell asleep.

"You know," Mary told me the next day, "a lot of girls went to the party. Even more than I thought."

Ouch. I wish she didn't know that. But I guess you can't expect eight-year-olds to keep this type of thing quiet. I still wonder if it was a mistake... Or if I should have called Susie's mother from a different room, and then told Mary that the email came...So much for twenty-twenty hindsight. Yet, now that it's over, I know that these types of experiences build character. Hard as it was, hopefully Mary will file it away and grow to become a more compassionate person.

Susie's Mother Speaks:

"Mommy, can I please have a birthday party this year? Everyone is doing them and it's so much fun, please..."

"Susie, let me speak to Daddy and get back to you. Remember, we make decisions by thinking about what's best for you not by what "everyone" does. And, I am not sure how we can possibly invite your whole grade- that is forty-five kids."

'Oh, Mommy no one invites the whole grade anymore. That is *so* last year. Everyone knows that it's just not done, and most kids get invited to at least some parties. Our gym teacher told us that we just have to be strong and not get insulted so easily. She does not like when we cry one bit. So I'm sure everyone will be just fine." She looked at me with her arms outstretched, sure that her logic would win out. Something still didn't feel right.

"Susie, something is not sitting right with me here and I will think about it and talk to Daddy. Your feelings are certainly very important to me. How do we know that the other eight-year-olds who hear about it will not be very hurt? You know how we always tell you that we have to care how we treat each other."

I decided that my husband would have good insight on the issue. "Daddy, Susie wants a birthday party this year and apparently, according to our sociology expert, one no longer needs to invite the whole grade as 'everyone' understands that with the recession, choosing some kids seems to be an acceptable option. Of course, I will double-check this with the principal, but assuming she has her facts correct, what do you think?"

"First of all, I can predict that my dear wife's heartstrings are tugging her very tightly worrying that she should not hurt anybody's feelings. Did I get that right? Great, can I please have the funds you would have handed to your life coach for that brilliant insight?" he laughed loudly, dispelling much of my tension.

"Okay, thanks for the laugh. But, seriously, how do we balance Susie's needs for a party with the very strong possibility that by excluding some kids, we are causing significant pain?"

"Listen, of course we don't want to hurt people. I think we need to trust that mature adults understand that there are limits in these kinds of activities, and knowing Susie's social challenges, preventing her from having the chance to participate may not be in her best interest. What did the principal say?"

"She said that in a school of this size, parents cannot be expected to invite all the kids, and that by inviting just a small group and not sending invitations in school, the kids need to learn to deal with disappointments. And, parents and teachers can help our kids learn these coping tools. Just like you were saying..."

"How do you manage to think so clearly without your heart confusing the issues?" I was always impressed by his levelheadedness, whereas sometimes my emotions got in the way.

"We tell Susie there are to be no invitations distributed at school in order to do our best to spare the feelings of the girls that are not invited. We also limit Susie to a maximum of five kids from each class so even if other students do learn of this party, they will recognize that it was only a small group that participated. Thirdly, we teach her not to talk about it in school. Fourthly, you need to relax and let Susie choose her five from each class, instead of you choosing her friends for her.

"Well, how did you know I was thinking of Mary and her mother and worrying about their sensitivity?"

"True, however we need to empower Susie to choose her close friends if this is to be a healthy social experience for her. It is not my belief that we need to force her to invite Mary as one of the girls in her inner circle. Remember what I said earlier about the life coach?"

"Yes."

"Go ahead and make an appointment. I have a feeling you will need to explore your own fears and insecurities around this issue before you can really help Susie socially integrate with her classmates. Remember, this party is about her needs not about our social choices."

"If you are logically right, why can I just picture Mary sobbing into her pillow with her mother rubbing her back, wondering what kind of parents exclude eight-year-olds from birthday parties?

"Anyway, thanks for this conversation and I will take out the mixer and start baking. Why don't I feel more excited about this?"

Porcupine Quills

MARLA SPEAKS / MOM SPEAKS

Marla Speaks:

I really relate to porcupines. There is something about a well-aimed barb from my mother-in-law that sets my quills from supine to upright. We had the dubious pleasure of hosting her recently, and the memory of her oft-related speech can still make me bristle, even though she is, once again, safe, well, and a plane ride away.

My husband is a teacher par excellence. He is knowledgeable and proficient in his field, a veritable expert after spending thirty years in the classroom. We were recently honored by the school; Sol, for his devoted years of service, and me, for my years of volunteer work on behalf of the school. That's what brought my mother-in-law to our home.

"He could've been anything, Marla," my mother-in-law began, and I heaved an inward sigh. I knew where this was going, and I nodded, wishing I still had a young baby whose wail would propel me away.

"He has such oratory gifts, and he's so smart! He was accepted to Columbia University. I'll only say it once (in this conversation, right, Mom?), Marla, but what a shame. Why, if he had finished his degree in law, he could have had it made. Dad built up the firm from scratch and established a whole clientele. He was respected and loved. People used to call him any time of day and night. Sol could have stepped right into his shoes (I thought they wear a different size) and taken over the entire business. They would have been waiting in line for him!"

And she shook her head ruefully, question marks dancing in her eyes at the incongruity of her dreams and real life.

I knew better than to argue, but those quills were poised.

"But Mom, this is what he wanted. Don't parents want their children to be happy and fulfilled?"

"Well yes, of course."

"So then what's the problem?"

"Oh, I don't know." She sighed emotionally, sliding a beautifully manicured hand through her perfectly coiffed hair. Her gold jewelry glinted as the sunlight hit it, and I studied her, simultaneously pitying her for her shallow values, while at the same time, wishing I could penetrate to her core and change her views.

"He could have been so successful (translation: rich). But," and another sigh, "He decided to marry young and designed some lofty dreams. (Right. It's all my fault. If he hadn't met me, perhaps he would have followed the trajectory of your dreams.) Then he became consumed by his dream of saving the world by educating its children- bah!

"How long until you get married?" She continued the saga, and I restrained myself from blurting out the familiar lines as I glanced back through the mists of time and my starry-eyed-self alongside my equally starry-eyed fiancé.

"Two months, he told us. It was a good thing I was sitting down, Marla. Oh, well. Life doesn't always turn out the way you want it to, does it?"

"No, Mom," I agreed, thinking of certain children who've caused me pain with their lifestyle choices. "It really doesn't."

As long as we're wishing for fairy tale endings, I wouldn't have minded supportive in-laws, in-laws who embraced our way of life, though different from theirs, in-laws who showed me that I am the daughter they always dreamed of welcoming into their family.

"So, Marla, I'm glad I came for him," she told me as I brought her to the airport on the day she left. "He only has one mother. I had to come, don't you see? How could I not?"

"But Mom," I finally protested, voicing the pain of my inner child, "didn't you come for me, too?"

Both of my parents died many years ago, and it seems that a child, even when grown, never loses the longing for her parents.

"Oh, but you had so many people," she replied, brushing off my yearning like a piece of lint on her fur coat. "You didn't need me."

So many people? You mean my one and only brother and our children, who traveled in for both of their parents? Why can there never be unconditional love, even after thirty years? Would it have hurt to say that you came for both of us? And that you were proud of our accomplishments?

Mom Speaks:

I know some people advise that when your children are adults, keep the mouth closed and the wallet open. Yet, as a mom who really cares about her family, there are certain things that are just too painful to observe quietly. Let's take my son, for example. Now, not just because he is my son, but everyone says he is brilliant, analytical, classy, and an incredible orator. I can just close my eyes and picture him successfully winning case after case in the courtroom as he masterfully shreds his opponent's arguments to crumbs. He actually received a scholarship to an Ivy League university, but he threw it away in order to save time and complete his degree within a shorter time frame, but in a less prestigious college. What was he thinking?

I know that we cannot rewrite history. I know he refused the scholarship and felt fulfilled when he embarked on his unique program to become a teacher, in addition to rashly deciding to marry his sweet wife when she was only eighteen years old. It was very hard then and still is; they're so, well, different from the rest of the family. Their clothing and manner of presenting themselves simply doesn't reflect our way of life. To be honest, I cover up that pain, but it still hurts. It's almost as though my child rejected the way of life we taught and chose something totally different. Yet, if not for my worry about them, I would really continue to hide my disappointment. Sometimes, it feels as though he was my baby yesterday, yet I know that my long-term memory seems to be in sharper focus than my short term. What do I hope to accomplish by rewinding their life story backwards thirty years?

I guess I really worry about their finances. They have a large family, and although they are beloved in their community, and I do have the most adorable grandchildren and great-grandchildren- it is so hard to see them struggle. I want to convey that I will not be here forever to support their way of life, and that my son needs to step up and support his large family. So, although in the past my wallet has been open wide and I never was much good at the closed mouth part, now I just feel a bit worried to continue giving. Perhaps reminding my talented son about his gifts could push him to go back to school and get a more lucrative profession. Many people return to school and make career shifts at his age...and he still looks so young and handsome...everyone says so!

For some reason, whenever we have these conversations, my daughter-in-law gets so defensive. But, wait, I am not trying to attack. Why does she defend herself from me- doesn't she realize I love her? Why, I am always bragging about my daughter-in-law who raised such a marvelous family.

I am still old fashioned enough to believe that it is my son's job to support her, and she has worked so hard raising these lovely children. She then makes these irrelevant comments about kids choosing their professions and finding fulfillment. What about dollars and cents? It costs a lot of money to provide for children. And the cost of living does not go down either. Sometimes when I hear her speak, she sounds like the starry-eyed, impractical eighteen-year-old that captured my son's heart so many years ago. She is a smart girl. Hasn't she learned that dreams are nice, but that living costs money?

And, yes, what if the time comes when we can no longer help them? What if we cannot afford to give them money because we will incur expenses that tend to come with old age? Maybe they do not realize that the way of nature is for parents to pass, and then I will no longer be able to help them.

I wish my daughter-in-law would understand the concern I have for their future and financial security. Maybe I will try to share my opinions just one more time. No one can ever say that I give up easily. Hey, maybe my orator of a son doesn't only inherit his brilliant skills from his father's side.

Koalas, Here We Come

EVIE SPEAKS / MOMMY SPEAKS

Evie Speaks:

"Wow, Australia? Jack, I know you've wanted to take the next step for a while, and the salary sounds like we can live with a bit more peace of mind. Visualizing palm trees and the ability for our children to enjoy the outdoors every day sounds like a dream." Yet, if there is so much blessing in this opportunity, why is my stomach contracting so tightly? And, why are the tears threatening to spill out in torrents?

"Evie, how can I thank you for standing by my side and encouraging me? I know it must be beyond painful to think about leaving your mother and traveling so far away. This is a joint decision. If it is too much to ask, then we will find another option. Together, we will figure something out."

"Jack, Mommy always said that if Daddy were alive, she would have followed him to the end of the earth. She probably did not realize that she would have to eat her words one day… Yes, she taught me that my place is by your side." Thinking about this made me feel more sure about this decision.

"Evie, let's do what we usually do when we're facing a significant decision. Let's write down the pros and cons, do a lot of investigative research and even a pilot trip, and then we'll be equipped to take the next step. And remember the research firm provides yearly trips to America, which we can treasure and utilize fully so that Mommy can enjoy her precious grandchildren. If it makes you feel any better, I love Mommy, too, and will miss her."

"Thanks, Jack. Let me call Stacey. She helps me see the big picture without being overwhelmed with emotions." I picked up the phone and prayed that my loyal friend would be available to answer. Her voice on the other line made me sigh with relief.

"Hi Stacey. How are you? What's new, you ask? Oh, same old, same old, just that Jack was accepted by a firm in Australia and my heart is breaking and feels torn between loyalty to my mother and to my husband. Yes, you heard correctly. Oh Stacey, what am I going to do? The guilt is overwhelming whatever I do. It feels like a lose-lose. Either I cause pain to my mother who has suffered tremendously throughout her life, or I disappoint my husband and interfere with the pursuit of his dreams. I know we will only have positive outcomes when I help my husband achieve his goals. My head may know that, but my heart is breaking."

"Evie, have you spoken to your mother yet?"

"No, I can't bring myself to call her. My stomach feels so tight, it reminds me of my most painful contractions."

"Take a deep breath. You're a wonderful person, and you love to please everyone and make them happy. It's really hard for you to inflict pain."

"That's right. Yet, some decisions, by their very nature, involve hurting at least one person. And, these are two of the most important relationships in my life."

"It must be incredibly difficult for you. Evie, can you find any benefit in this challenge? You often say that tests are given to us to help us grow."

"Maybe I will have to find other creative ways to reach out to my mother that I would not have done from a closer proximity. Maybe supporting my husband's dreams will help him grow in ways that are way beyond what he can achieve here. Maybe the unity Jack and I will attain will create a more secure home environment for our children."

"You're doing really well. How are those contractions as we speak now?"

"Definitely quieter and I'm breathing more deeply. Stacey, how can I thank you?"

"Isn't that what friends are for? This is tough. But I've never seen a tough situation stop you from proceeding with optimism and purpose. I noticed that you did not mention the possibilities of your own individual growth and developing your gifts. You've always dreamed of teaching high school. Maybe doors will open there, too. And one more thing: Call your mother and have that conversation. She wants you to be at your husband's side. I have no doubt." I hung up with much of my confusion and guilt resolved. I knew that once I spoke to my mother, I would be able to move forward.

"Jack, what did the firm say about bringing our furniture? And, can you get me a few numbers of families who live there so I can find out about schools and life style expectations and maybe some job possibilities?"

"Phew! Looks like I have my happy wife back. I know this will be good for all of us somehow."

"Thanks for understanding my challenge and being patient with me. And can you call the travel agent and book our first trip back? I know that seems funny before we even get there.

Yet just knowing we have a date to see Mommy again may help both of us in handling this transition. I'm calling Mommy now to share the news. Maybe prayer would help at a time like this." Pausing for a moment, I sent up a quick entreaty to Someone I knew was listening from on high. With trembling fingers, I dialed the number, hoping that my newfound positivity would make this easier. "Hi, Mommy…"

Mommy Speaks:

"Oh, hi, Evie, how are you? How're the kids?"

I was washing dishes when my eldest daughter called, but decided to take a break and relax on the couch while we chatted.

Living in Philadelphia while my two married daughters live in Cleveland is challenging, so I try to keep our phone call time sacrosanct. I've been a widow for nearly twenty years, and the girls are all I have.

"You have some news for me? Okay, I'm all ears. You're moving? Oh, where to? AUSTRALIA? Why not the moon? That may be closer. But," I could hardly choke the words out, "WHY ON EARTH ARE YOU GOING THERE?"

"Jack found a great business opportunity with a firm that he really likes there. He has been searching for a growth opportunity for a long time- you know he's felt stifled in his current position, right? This is the perfect chance for him to stretch his wings."

I was quiet for a while, but after the silence stretched uncomfortably long between us, Evie ventured a tentative, "Ma? Are you there?"

"Sort of," I said quietly. "You know, as much as I don't want you to move overseas and limit the time we see each other even more than it is already, I have to tell you something. If Daddy were still here," I paused, swallowing the lump that just formed in my throat, "I would follow him to the ends of the earth. That's what a wife is supposed to do- support her husband. So, much as I don't want you to go- are you sure you can't find a job any closer where Jack can be satisfied? Aha, you've looked everywhere...Well, then," I had to pause again- that lump was growing into a mountain- "I give you my blessing. You're doing the right thing."

"Oh, Mommy!" Evie cried out, and I reached for some tissues as tears cascaded down my cheeks. Taking hold of herself, she continued talking while I listened, sniffed, and dabbed. "This is so hard. I don't want to move this far away. But Jack's been looking for a long time now. This job has exactly what he's been looking for. It's such a fantastic opportunity. And we'll come in the summer to visit before we go, okay? I love you..."

"A visit will be terrific!" I fought like a valiant soldier to inject enthusiasm into my voice. "That will be something to look forward to."

Our conversation veered to the kids and their antics, and I heard myself laugh at appropriate moments. But my mind was far away...

Australia? I stared blankly at the phone once our call was over. When will I see her again? I don't have money for that kind of trip. I can barely afford to pay my bills on my small secretary's salary. How does a mother say good-bye to her daughter and not know the next time they'll see each other? And Evie and Jack certainly don't have money for trips back to the states. Well, at least there's the phone. I'm going to call AT&T and find out how much it will be to call Australia.

"How much?" Aghast, I hung up the receiver, and burst into a fresh gale of tears. So I won't even be able to call her very often either- it costs a small fortune! Not only that, but there's a fourteen hour time difference! Oh, dear G-d- don't I have enough challenges in my life? My husband is gone and has been for a lifetime, I don't have money, which makes everything so much more difficult, and now Evie is leaving me. How will I cope? Why did I tell her she has my blessing? Can I retract? No, Judy, you did the right thing. A mother is supposed to let her daughter spread her wings and not burden her with guilt. But if it's the right thing, why is it so hard?

Meet Your New Grandson

MOM SPEAKS / SALLY SPEAKS

Mom Speaks:

"Meet your new grandson," flashed on my cell phone screen alongside a magnificent picture of a beautiful new baby boy.

"Congratulations!" I shouted to the friend sitting beside me, jumping up from my chair as I stared at the picture in wonder. "Howie and Sally had a boy!"

"Congratulations!" She hugged me, and I grabbed my pocketbook and prepared to leave. Who had patience to sit through a lengthy speech when our long awaited bundle had finally arrived? I must call everyone, the children, my sister, my in-laws and close friends. I longed to reach through the phone and kiss the silken cheek of our family's newest member, and I could hardly wait to share in this poignant and precious moment.

I paused for an emotional moment to reflect. How much effort it took for us to reach this sublime moment! Allow me to explain. Howie and his siblings became my children in a unique and special way. When Howie was ten, I had married his widowed father, becoming what the world disparagingly calls a stepmother. Disregarding the negative connotation, I wholeheartedly embraced him and his sisters as my children, determined to become their mother. It took years of patience and love, monumental effort, and rivers of privately shed tears, but we finally breached the chasm that separated us. By the time Howie left for college, he was finally calling me Ma, and my heart rejoiced. As the eldest, Howie set the tone. Once he accepted me as his mother, his sisters followed suit.

But enough journeying back in the past- we have a trip to prepare for! Maybe we should stay over the weekend? After all, since Howie and Sally live a plane ride away, how often do we spend quality time together? Once we're going, we may as well turn it into special family time and bond with our newest addition.

I bounced the idea off of Howie, awaiting his reaction. Surely he would want us there with open arms to share in this beautiful time.

"Well, my in laws will be here, and Sally needs a lot of rest. Too many people at one time might not give her that opportunity." Silence. Aha. So we're not wanted. Could it be because, after all's said and done, I'm still only a stepmother? After all these years, has the barrier I thought we overcame returned to haunt me? Or are we really wanted, and perhaps I misunderstood? Confusion whirled within me, so I consulted with my sister (it comes in handy to have a mental health counselor in the family) as to the best way to make my proposal. I wound up carefully trying to follow Sylvia's admonishments, telling Howie a message without allowing the pain to seep through, and just doing my best to be there for the two of them in whatever capacity they needed. Sylvia told me not to just consider solving this short-term problem, but to think about this relationship as one for life.

"We just want you to be happy," I pushed the words from my lips, hoping Howie couldn't hear the pain pulsing beneath the veneer. Or maybe part of me wished he would hear it? "Daddy and I will come in for the day, and if you'd like us to stay for the weekend, fine. If it's not the right time, and you and Sally need privacy, that's fine, too. We'll just slip in and out; we really just want to meet him, you know, congratulate you in person (really now, what's a few thousand miles between family anyway?). Be honest, please, and let us know what you want. Whatever's good for you is good for us."

It took a day of silence for me to infer that they didn't want to tell us straight out not to stay longer than a day, but we got the unspoken message. We needed to book our tickets, and I still wanted absolute clarity before making the final decision. Later I found that my son had indeed responded via a text (I had dreamt of a conversation), and yes, it would be better to just slip in and out. I couldn't help but wonder- would he have rejected me if he were my flesh and blood? Does a real son ever tell his mother not to come, especially when there's a precious new grandson on the scene?

Ouch- it really hurts. To be unwanted at such a milestone in my children's lives feels like a hornet plunging its stinger deeper and deeper into the fabric of my soul. Now, Self, I counseled, you know you're being unreasonable. They just had a baby, and you don't want to be in the way. At least they're being honest! Would you have wanted to stay on if you were not really wanted? But then the other voice countered. Me? In the way? I would help- I would do whatever they wanted, from cooking to cleaning to holding that beautiful baby and anything in between. Me? A hindrance? We're your parents, after all- yes, I am, too, Howard. Don't you remember, my Howie? I helped you with homework, took you to doctors, soothed your fears, listened to your concerns, bandaged your bruises, cheered you on at your sports games...I mothered you, Howie. And how often do we see you- don't you want to see us?

I prayed whole-heartedly for you to have this joy for so many years. While you waited for your arms to be filled, I felt your aching pain with every fiber of my being. And now- I've been rebuffed. That's the way it is- it's the new generation. In my day, no one asked me how long they could stay or if it was a convenient time when they planned a visit. My in-laws just gave us their itinerary, and I smiled and tried to be a good daughter-in-law, even when it was hard.

Howie sent me some gorgeous pictures this morning, and my heart melted when I saw him holding his new son. What a miracle- a beautiful, healthy baby. Howie, my Howie, a father.

I called a few days later just to check in and ask how they were doing.

"Where are you staying?" Sally asked, and I told her we'd stay at a nearby hotel.

"Oh, that's nice," she said, "and what are your plans in the end?"

When I explained that it didn't sound like the best time for us to hang around, so we would just zip in and out, she agreed. "Yeah, sounds good. Maybe another time, Ma."

Yeah. Maybe...

If only Howie had called and assured us that he would have loved for us to stay longer, but Sally was not feeling well, perhaps the pain wouldn't be as raw. Any excuse would have made me feel better instead of feeling rejected.

Well, we came and went, and I left a piece of my heart behind with my new grandson. At least I held him for a few hours. And in the blink of an eye, as if the visit had been a dream, we were home again, separated by a gaping chasm, and I wondered when we would all spend some real time together. Certainly not any time soon- that was clear. Now, now, Self, stop being bitter. This was the right move and you know it. Sigh.

I love you, Howie and Sally. Raise him well. After all, he is my grandson...

Sally Speaks:

My body feels so drained and utterly exhausted in a way that I never experienced before. Obsessed with the idea of sleeping, my brain cannot even contemplate anything more complex than the following one-syllable words when the phone rings.

"Hi, Mom-You- want- to- come- stay- with- us- now- Oh- I- see- well- that's- nice- and- we'll –get- back- to- you- soon.- Bye- have- a- nice- day."

I proceeded to close my eyes once again and drift off into blissful sleep when suddenly the sounds of a newborn baby crying pierced through the hazy webs of confusion where until three days ago a sharp brain used to dwell.

Baby, whose baby is crying? After years of hopeful yearning, is this little one actually ours? Why, then, do I not feel anything except numbness? When I attempt to shake it off, anxiety seems to take its place, which feels even worse. How will I have the stamina to take care of this helpless little person when I lack the energy to walk from the bedroom to the kitchen? And why do I just feel like crying? A primal, inexplicable need for my mother to take care of me fills me with a sense of utter dependency.

Somewhere in the deep recesses of my mind, something seems wrong with this picture. Everyone else is smiling and crying from joy. I certainly already love this little person. But, can Howie just ask everyone to turn off the noise and call my mother?

"Yes, Howie, what's going on? Your parents want to come to see the baby? This weekend? They want to help. Howie, I like your parents very much and I do not want to hurt your mother. She is a very kind and sensitive woman. But, I can't right now. I do not even feel like myself physically or emotionally.

"I am sure you will find a way to explain to them and they will understand that a girl just needs her mother, especially after a first child. None of the childbirth classes prepared me for how sore and achy I feel all over. When the baby is ready to sleep, I spend the time rolling from one uncomfortable position to the next, trying to find relief. As comfortable as I am with your family, there is still a feeling of wanting to be at my best when they're around, and right now, I do not even feel like me.

"Your mother had children; I am sure she must understand my state of body and mind better than most people.

"Thanks, Howie, I mean, Daddy, for understanding, and can you please dim the lights on your way out so I can get some sleep? It's hard to imagine ever feeling alert and energetic again. Tell your mother to come another time. She really is such a wonderful lady."

Surprise Package

RACHEL SPEAKS / EILEEN SPEAKS

Rachel Speaks:

The big, brown, ubiquitous UPS truck rumbled to a stop right outside our modest ranch home. Within a moment, all of my children and I converged from different sections of the house, gathering at the living room bay window to see what was coming our way. We held our collective breath as the truck opened its cavernous mouth, and an intrepid UPS veteran bore a bulky package aloft until he deposited it at our doorstep. With a jaunty wave, he was gone, and in a superb display of teamwork, we panted and lugged the big package into our kitchen.

"What could it be?" Judy asked.

"It's from Grandma," Becky announced, noticing the return address.

Armed with a kitchen scissors and steely determination, I broke through the layers of packing tape and opened the box. Thousands of peanuts greeted my eyes, and I sighed as they spilled over my floor while I reached down to find what was inside. Finally, I saw it. A big, brown archaic serving bowl, looking like it came right out of *Little House on the Prairie*. Just to give you an insider's glimpse, I detest shopping, and would have to seriously debate, if given the choice, whether I would prefer going to a medical appointment verses spending a few hours on this oh-so-feminine pastime. My mother-in-law, however, firmly believes in shopping as a significant, housewifely occupation, filling her home and ours with the products of her obsession. Thankfully we live in different cities. However, even I have some taste preferences, and this bowl was definitely not one of them.

"Hey, there's another one!" Joey shouted, his arms completely submerged inside the peanuts. Triumphantly, he withdrew another cellophane wrapped colonial style brown piece with large handles on each side, only this one was in pieces. I sighed with relief. *At least I would only have to keep one such bowl.*

"Thank you for the present," my husband called his mother later that evening.

"Oh, I'm so glad you like it," she enthused. "Isn't it a great set?"

A firm believer in the values of honesty, my husband made his first blunder.

"It's very nice, but the bowl with handles was broken."

"Broken?" my mother-in-law was shocked and upset. "I wonder how that happened. I told them to wrap it well."

Up went the unbroken relic to take its honorable place on an attic shelf (to be taken down and used the next time Mom visits), while its broken mate went into the garbage. Naïve, I assumed the story was over.

Several days later, the UPS truck was back. Warily, I watched our new friend (same guy- he gave us a smile this time) make the trek again from the back of his truck to our front door. For some reason, I wasn't surprised to see my in-laws' return address on the outside of the box, and my heart plummeted. Reaching inside the ubiquitous peanuts, I extracted the same bowl, only this time it was in even more pieces than the first one.

"So, do you love it?" Mom asked me as I rolled my eyes and cradled the receiver between my neck and ear.

"Thank you," I replied evasively. "But this one came broken, too."

Mom was not to be deterred. UPS came by several more times over the next few weeks. Each time I saw the truck, my eyes began to water; I wasn't sure whether to laugh or cry, so I did a little of both.

Finally, the day arrived. A package came, covered in even more peanuts and thicker layers of cellophane. Ever so carefully I reached inside and withdrew the earthenware serving bowl with large handles on either side; it was massive, it was brown, it was oval shaped, and it certainly would not fit into any of my kitchen cabinets.

"You did it!" my husband told his mother.

"Hurray!" she crowed. "Just enjoy it."

I grabbed the bowl and heaved my way up the attic steps.

"There," I told the original piece. "At least you have company," and I set it firmly beside its counterpart.

Several years passed, and every so often, our family was treated to a surprise package. A plate whose designer must have received a prize for originality, a three part crock pot set that takes up an entire counter, but each individual crock pot only holds one and a quarter quarts. *Well, considering the kids' appetites, that could feed about half of us at a time,* I mused, grateful to have attic storage. A big, beautiful silver coffee tureen that will keep your coffee warm for hours...just what I always wanted and needed- I just never realized.

My most recent package arrived this past Friday. Uh-oh. I turned to my cleaning lady, and we exchanged grins. She's been with us for years, so she's seen her share of packages.

"Here goes," I exclaimed, and she held her sides, laughing, watching, and waiting.

"One solid bamboo cutting board with a drip tray," I read, grunting as I placed the large, heavy board on my table. "Just what I always wanted."

And then came the box inside the box.

"A roasting rack." I stared at the metal rack, and it looked back at me wordlessly.

"Now exactly what do I do with this?" I turned to my cleaning lady who was now doubled over; her entire body convulsed with laughter.

"I don't know, Rachel. But when you find out, you let me know," she gasped.

I erupted in sidesplitting laughter, enjoying the freedom to just laugh and enjoy life.

Thanks, Mom. That was just what I needed.

Eileen Speaks:

"Good morning, Harry. Would you mind getting me a copy of the Sunday sales on your way back from walking the dog? You know how I love to save money and maybe I can find something for that hardworking daughter-in-law of mine. They live with the bare minimum, yet I love to decorate her home with lovely, stylish items."

"Now, Eileen, do you think they have anywhere left to put more decorations? Their kids do take up a lot of space."

I laughed. "Listen, Harry, trust me, a woman loves pretty things. Didn't our son, the doctor, quote a medical journal saying that a man needs to buy something pretty for his wife every three months?"

This argument was foolproof. He had to agree with me. Besides, this daughter-in-law is so complex, I never know if what I say pleases her or brings tears. When it comes to shopping, that is my area of expertise. I know that no woman can resist pretty gifts, and making her happy is also a way of giving to our son.

"So, now that we have determined the facts on the table, I can't wait to see the sales! Thanks for bringing the info back for me. Facts on the table…hmmm, that's it! Magnificent salad bowls to grace the table. Maybe Rachel thinks that I didn't notice, but those disposable salad bowls from the dollar store have got to go. Ugggh, how utterly tasteless! I will very tactfully mention it to her in our next conversation. I would not want guests to think that they lack class. What happens when prospective clients are invited over for dinner? I shudder to think of the potential consequences if she continues to use these bowls. Harry will be so proud of my extra sensitivity and how hard I work to be a mother, not just a mother-in-law, to Rachel. Okay, Eileen, off to your favorite past time-destination- MALL! Objective: new salad bowls for Mark and Rachel."

Shopping is so exhilarating. Maybe I should invite her to join me and give her a chance to get out. She would love it. So many pretty things to choose from…

Let's see- huge salad bowls. That should feed their family. Such lovely, dainty crockpots for their stew. I know some of their kids like potatoes and others do not, so this allows for differentiation. Eileen, you are one okay grandma, you even know the buzzwords in education today. I wonder why more people don't call for child rearing advice.

It's not easy to be a long distance grandmother, but modeling generosity cannot hurt for now or even when I am no longer here so they can remember me fondly.

Distraction time, so many salad bowls to choose from, and price is not even a factor when it comes to those darling children. Just beauty, good quality, name brand, and usefulness. And, some of the more overweight children could use a bit more salad and a bit less other stuff. I must advise Rachel about nutrition tips for her kids. It's hard to imagine what she'd do without my help and advice.

"Ma'am, could you please wrap this up to ensure there is no breakage? These bowls have a very special purpose and need to be shipped quite some distance. I expect that the store will take full responsibility for these items to arrive safely."

You know, I used to feel a bit ashamed of my penchant for shopping. It does seem a bit frivolous on the surface. But, now that I've matured, I recognize that there are limitless opportunities to give to my children. This week salad bowls and next week, a varied crock pot set. The possibilities are endless.

"Do you think Rachel even knows how lucky she is? Maybe I should let her know in our next conversation. Don't worry, Harry, I will say it tactfully, always tactfully."

I knew that they would get the gift within a week. I didn't wait for them to call; I was too excited to hear Rachel's reaction. "So, kids, how are you enjoying the new stunning salad bowls? Bet you never saw anything like them before, right? Did you say they came broken? Why, that is absolutely unforgivable. I will go straight back to the mall and have them reship a brand new set. I don't have to, you say. I would not have it any other way. When it comes to you kids, nothing is too difficult.

"Rachel, you know, in life we have to be assertive to make things happen. Just wait till I say my piece to the manager. No children of mine will EVER receive broken shards again."

Tentacles of Fear

SHELLY SPEAKS / MOM SPEAKS

Shelly Speaks:

Tentacles of fear and sadness gripped my heart as I watched my beloved father-in-law struggle to get up from his chair and perform other everyday functions, like eating, reaching, and following a conversation. It seemed clear that his physical weakness stemmed from the cruel dementia that has taken up residence in his once fertile and rich mind. You could almost see, perhaps from the vacant look in his eyes, that his brain was refusing to send signals to his body, and therefore his limbs refused to perform. I've always cherished our special relationship, and seeing his deterioration was excruciatingly painful. Having grown up without a father, my heart swelled every time he would tell me that I'm like a daughter to him. Invariably I would respond that he, too, is like a father to me.

    How can it be, I wondered, that a brilliant, philosophical, successful attorney can become a shadow of himself? Dad, I sometimes want to shout- you can beat this! Don't let it get you- you're too good, too smart, too everything. And then the tears come...

Mom (my mother-in-law) gives me periodic updates by phone, telling me that he can't button his shirts or tie his tie, he needs help dressing, or says something nonsensical. My heart clenches with a physical pain as I listen, and sometimes she cries.

"He was so smart, Shelly," she says, "It seems like this disease picks the smart ones."

Hmm. I mull that one over. Exactly how high does one's IQ have to be in order to qualify?

"Mom is overwhelmed," I tell my husband. "It's really too much for an eighty-two year old woman to be a 24/7 nurse. Dad needs help at night, too. Can't we do something?" The assisted living home where they live only offers help in an emergency, but a person has to be independent in caring for his own daily needs.

But they weren't ready for our help. Mom insisted on caring for Dad, even though she complained often that it was too hard for her. So I listened, empathized, and felt frustrated and helpless against the tide of an increasingly debilitating situation. Then, suddenly, in one day everything changed. Mom called us later to inform us of what happened.

"Mark," Mom said to Dad, startled, "Why are you babbling? And what's wrong with your shoulder? Why is one side higher than the other?"

A nurse hurried to call an ambulance, and Dad was rushed off to the hospital. After several days of testing, the reports came back that he had not suffered a stroke- they were not sure what caused his sudden deterioration- and he was sent to rehab for several weeks. And then came the crash. Dad was no longer eligible to live with Mom in assisted living- he didn't even meet the criteria for their memory care unit- and had to live elsewhere.

When I called him in his new residence, my heart broke into a thousand shards as I heard his familiar deep tenor. He told me, "I miss my wife. I don't understand why I can't be with her."

"I'm sorry, Dad," I empathized, fighting back a tidal wave of emotion. "That's really rough. But she comes every day, right?"

"No," he answered emphatically. "I can't remember the last time I saw her."

I knew she had just been there yesterday.

Wanting to support Mom, I called to check in and absorbed the volumes of her pain.

"Going down to meals without him is so painful," she cried. "I miss him so much, and all the other couples sit together- except…"

"This is not a viable solution," I told my husband. "We've got to get him back with her somehow. It's just so wrong. How do you separate a husband and wife of so many years?"

My idea of hiring help was rejected- deemed too costly- so I racked my brains for an idea. I decided to send her an email.

Dear Mom,

Since Dad is walking now, do you think your facility would reevaluate his condition and perhaps allow him to move back with you? I'm happy to call them and arrange for the evaluation.

The response came shortly.

Shelly, I feel bad that you think I'm not capable of getting him reevaluated. I took care of all his needs, handle all the bills, and take the bus to see him every day…besides, he can't come back here. Hiring 24/7 help is too expensive. That's why I just moved to a small suite, to save money.

Oh no, she took my message the wrong way. I quickly typed a response.

Dear Mom,

You are immensely capable and have done a super-amazing job in caring for Dad. We live so far away and love you both so much. My intention in suggesting that I make the arrangement stemmed from caring and a desire to help. You've handled this whole situation valiantly by yourself, and I was hoping to assist, only because I love you. I'm sorry you thought I meant anything else.

Love,

Shelly

The dynamics of this mother-in-law-daughter-in-law relationship never fail to amaze me. You can have the best of intentions, say and do everything right, but somehow your motives are always suspect.

Mom Speaks:

Tentacles of fear gripped my heart as the nurses came and took away my partner in life. They murmured some platitudes that did not even penetrate about how the new place is so much more convenient and able to provide for all of his needs, and of course I could visit him daily. What do they understand about separating a wife from her husband of over fifty years? Visitations? Is this the end of our dreams of caring for each other throughout old age?

Oh, the relentless guilt. Its cumbersome waves wash over me as my inner critic loudly berates me for worrying about my own loneliness. What about your husband who was once so smart, capable and a support system to the entire family? Why are you just selfishly thinking about yourself? He must be petrified and confused as he slips in and out of lucid moments, wondering why his wife abandoned him when he needs her most.

At least my own brain seems to function. I take comfort in my independence and ability to take care of the finances, meal planning, and all of our medical needs. It is vitally important to me to put on a tough front for my children. If they would ever suspect my limitations and vulnerabilities, maybe I would also have to live out my years with patients suffering from Dementia, Alzheimer's, and every other kind of mental deterioration. No matter what, I will maintain an upper lip in front of my kids. Be strong, honey, be strong.

As a young child, old age always scared me. My sister loved to visit old age homes, but I could not handle seeing the once vibrant people looking like shadows of themselves with hardly the energy to stand on their own two feet. I remember going with my class in 8th grade to a nursing home and seeing an old lady screaming from a wheelchair. It looked like she was staring at me, yet when I got closer, she was not focused on me at all- just screaming strings of words. I ran back shaking to the school bus and waited for the other students to return. Now, my own husband is living in that same kind of institution, and I am terrified that it could happen to me.

Judging from the recent email conversation I just had with my daughter in law, I am worried that my children already doubt my ability to cope. What are they thinking after all that I have done and continue to do? Why is my daughter in law suggesting that she will organize an evaluation for my husband? They think I am losing it! I am not losing it.

Shattered Dreams

ANN SPEAKS / ALBERT SPEAKS

Ann Speaks:

Young and idealistic, I married and dreamed of supporting my husband, a perpetual student, who delighted in researching ancient literature. What better foundation for the beginning of our marriage than altruism? I would work with love, becoming his loyal partner as my husband toiled day and night. I was thrilled to help him achieve his goals...

Music played, vows were exchanged, and amid resounding "I do's" and ecstatic dancing, my dreams began to play out. We settled into our apartment, and soon after I landed a job as a nurse in a local hospital, thankful for a hopeful beginning. But the hours were long, the work intense, and somehow, in addition to my twelve hour shifts, I had to muster the strength to take care of the house and prepare dinners, served with a smile, please. And then our precious baby entered the scene. I was in a cyclonic whirlwind of tension and overwhelmed as I raced from work to the babysitter, trying to pacify the baby and put up dinner at the same time. Often when the baby's cries escalated, my tears joined his and we cried together.

Yet when Albert came home, I pulled myself together, put a warm smile on my face, and made sure that he never fathomed my internal upheaval. I was managing fine, thank you, and it was my pleasure and privilege to support his endeavors. Yet, if this was so heavenly sublime, why did I feel like I was slowly unraveling, piece by piece?

By the time baby number two announced her arrival, dinner had become a hurried and simple affair, the house was in constant shambles, and I felt like I was constantly panting my way up a steep precipice, yet never reaching the longed for peak. I had no social life (who had the time or energy?) and I was tired. So very tired.

"Albert," I timidly ventured, shuddering as I dipped my toes into frigid waters, "I think I need to cut back on my hours. I'm just- not- managing. And I wondered, I mean, would it be possible for you to stay home at night instead of going to the library to study?"

The complete look of shock on Albert's face made me want to tuck my head and toes into a shell and never come out. His expression showed disillusionment, betrayal, and pain- the loss of a dream. How could I do this to him, his eyes cried, after three years of school? We had talked long term, committed to the goal- I had promised. And now, just when he mired too deep to just emerge and shake off the droplets, just when he was starting to achieve his goals and make real progress, I was complicating matters. What kind of wimp was I anyway? And why does it seem like the rest of the women's workforce worldwide manage their loads with ease and dignity while I was struggling under my miniscule burden? How could I do this to him? Would I be able to live with myself knowing I wasn't living up to the commitment I made? Maybe I should keep pushing myself and ignore my feelings. After all, a promise is a promise.

"Maybe you're just having a hard day," Albert finally said in response to my query. "The baby's been teething…"

When he said those words, I realized that I could continue pretending, but somewhere along the line it would backfire. He wouldn't have the same wife he married, but rather a robotic shadow performing the motions. And that's when the dam broke and the floodgates were unleashed.

"No," I sobbed, "it's not just a day or two or even a week. I haven't managed since Joey was born, and now that Anita's here, my life feels like a nightmare. I'm sorry, Albert, I really am. I wanted this to work so badly. I was totally committed to this ideal. But," I choked in a whisper, "I can't do this anymore. I'm really sorry."

Albert Speaks:

So many people focus on the challenges facing women in today's workforce. Somehow they are expected to appear professional as they hold down full time jobs, yet they are also expected to keep tidy homes and be devoted wives and mothers. Before looking for my life partner, I knew I had to find a gem, someone truly special who would share in my dreams and walk alongside me, helping me to realize them.

Usually, my first dates were rather neutral. With Annie, there was a palpable excitement in the air as we practically anticipated each other's opinions and enjoyed the time together as the minutes flew by. After several months of dating, we both knew that it was just a matter of time before we became an officially engaged couple. Smooth was not the word; we were both delighted at the seamless transition from "if" to "when" and from "I" to "we". We discussed the expected topics of goals and where we each see ourselves in five years and ten years, smiling knowingly as our dreams coincided. It was as though we had rehearsed a prearranged script. Mom and Dad were thrilled. My finance's family was ecstatic, as well. Why not? They just got the catch of the century, all modesty aside. And I felt so grateful to have such a wonderful fiancé. We began to dream together.

Married life with Annie was even better than I envisioned. I maintained my rigorous study schedule and she took obvious pride in my achievements. The qualitative difference it made to my studies to have a personal coach encouraging me propelled me forward in ways that caused both my peers and professors to marvel. Wellsprings of new understandings just seemed to bubble out from the recesses of my mind. I felt grateful every day for the ideal life partner who wanted nothing more than for her husband to excel and publish his research.

Recently, however, I noticed that something felt different in the atmosphere when I came home at night. Although Annie continued to greet me with a smile, there was an unfamiliar strained look peeking out from underneath the smile, almost as if the smile felt forced. When I asked her if everything was okay, she reverted quickly to sharing the antics of our children and the interesting events at work in her normal, bubbly way, and I attributed the earlier furrow to women's moods.

Later that week, the bubble burst. My dear wife, Annie, spilled out her heart. She was completely overwhelmed, and the reality of her responsibilities far exceeded anything she pictured when I was applying to my graduate program. Her tears cascaded down her face and I felt terrible knowing she had been suffering, yet felt that the rug was being pulled out from under me. Were my dreams about to evaporate like a puff of smoke?

Our first long talk definitely would not be endorsed by leading marriage experts. We were both talking and focused on our own pain and no one was listening. I told her I would speak to my mentor and we would come to a solution together. Then, I escaped to my library, my haven, away from the guilt provoking intensity of her tears. Much to my surprise, my own tears poured forth as I confided in my mentor about the recent events. I had so many goals. Why, after completing my dissertation, I imagined immersion in post-doctorate study. I lived and breathed for the atmosphere of growing in my research, feeling that each new nugget of information was furthering me in my endeavor. Furthermore, what happened to our shared dream? I resolved to be more sympathetic to my wife, but the thought of giving up my aspirations disrupted my good intentions. Annie apologized and life continued as normal. I helped out more and hoped it was just a passing phase. For the next six months, we talked about everything except for this unspoken topic, which was foremost on both of our minds. However, I could no longer ignore her obvious exhaustion or the long shadows under her eyes.

At the end of the day, do I want my dreams fulfilled if they become my wife's nightmares and they come at the expense of her physical and emotional health? Annie told me she feels terrible, but that she just cannot manage and her strength is waning. She deeply wanted me to pursue my studies with true sincerity.

I can choose to be resentful and play the blame game. I can choose to accept this as direction from a higher power. Maybe G-d wants a different type of service plan than the one I envisioned. I can continue pursuing my love of literature. Annie and I both want that. But I can also take financial pressure off of my wife by contributing to the family finances. Perhaps I can land a part time job teaching literature analysis. It will be difficult, particularly as I watch my fellow students complete their courses faster than I will be able to. Yet I am certain that I will not lose in any way by being a better husband and father. It's time for me to comfort Annie who has been tormenting herself.

Annie, what do you think about me working part time so you can cut down on your hours? And, Annie, I want you to have an early night tonight while I study at home. You need some rest.

Yikes Mom's Moving In!

STEPHANIE SPEAKS / ALLEN SPEAKS

Stephanie Speaks:

Shaking my head to clear any possible obstruction, I'm wondering if my ears heard correctly. Did Allen just ask me if I would be open to his mother moving in with us? He's not serious, is he? But one look at his expression assured me he was quite serious and anxiously awaiting my response.

"Allen, I'd love to be a saint and say yes, but you know how rocky my relationship with Mom has always been, growing more so as she ages. I'm concerned that I'm not up to the challenge."

Allen was quiet and just looked at me steadily. The silence was deafening.

"I know what you're thinking. After all we owe our parents, how dare I even consider saying no? But isn't my sanity worth something?"

Allen exhaled loudly. "Just think about it," he asked, and with great reluctance, I agreed.

Mom moving in- what would that do to my life? Well, for one, I would probably be late to almost every place I tried to go.

Dad used to joke that Mom had two speeds: slow and very slow. She tends to remember things precisely at the time we're supposed to leave. The second problem is her incessant talking. I am an introvert, at least partially so, and I thrive on introspection and periods of silence. If she talked to me all day, Allen could just commit me. Hey, then we wouldn't have such a space issue- there would be one less person in the house. Mom also tends to be very critical, especially if there is an overweight child in the house or if anyone doesn't do something appropriate for his or her physical health. "It doesn't hurt to be good looking," is her credo that she spouts at frequent intervals, and G-d should save the one who doesn't aspire to look their very best while in my mother-in-law's presence. I have one child who is overweight; if she ever sees him enjoying food that he "shouldn't" have, he's in dire straits. Mom shows her concern and love by grabbing food out of his hands, explaining the risks of being overweight while tears gather in his eyes.

"Do you want to have a heart attack or get diabetes?" she asks, fire flashing from her eyes.

I have another who's not a great tooth brusher and needs reminders. The last time Mom visited, she gave this child an hour long lecture on tooth brushing, how her teeth should look as white as a sheet, how disappointed she is…So the mental health of my entire family is at stake if we go ahead with this insane plan.

I propose finding a good assisted living home in our vicinity, and we'll visit her frequently. As I imagine proposing this option to Allen, I feel pricks of guilt pierce my heart. After all, she is his mother and my mother-in-law, which equals an obligation. So many people make this sacrifice with love and devotion. I don't know how they find the inner strength- I guess I'm a selfish narcissist. Should I say yes?

Allen Speaks:

It's hard to believe that I, Mr. Practical, cerebral, logical and the rest of the nicknames that typify my lack of emotionalism, feel literally torn apart by this recent role reversal in our lives. My opinionated, strong mother has suddenly become so vulnerable, terrified to be on her own, insecure in decision making, and very needy. Heart muscles that successfully avoided working out for years, never experiencing tears and pain, are being challenged to face this reality while failing miserably at this task.

My wife, who has begged me for years not to fix but just to listen and validate, does not recognize her new, teary, reflective husband worrying about his lonely mother. It probably does not help our relationship that she sees my mother as the main beneficiary of this newly discovered tenderness, particularly as their connection has been strained to its limits throughout our marriage.

My mother communicates directly, some may even call it blunt, yet to me, this is just Mom talking. She has strong opinions about everything, ranging from appearance, style, household decoration and child rearing, and loves to share them with my wife. My wife's middle name is sensitive, and accordingly she takes great offense at my mother's perceived interference and lack of tact, particularly when it appears to be directly targeted to one of our children. I give my wife a lot of credit for her efforts over the years in hosting and welcoming my mother despite the anguish she suffers before, during, and after every visit. Have I ever told her, you ask? No, the old me may not even have noticed, much less mentioned a word. Hmmm-more food for reflection-what is happening to me?

Over the years, I watched from afar as a number of my slightly older peers have placed their parents into elder care facilities. I disdained their choice, feeling it was a dishonorable way to treat their parents. But now that it's becoming pertinent, imagining my kids running around while my elderly mother craves peace and quiet creates a different picture in my mind.

Ambivalence- what a tortuous state. Part of me wants to take in my mother and care for her. I love her. She gave birth to me and raised me. Yet, another part of me sees the storm I would be setting off in my own home. How can I even ask this of my wife? Yes, I know she is kind and runs a volunteer organization for elderly people almost singlehandedly. But her home is her refuge. She writes actively and finally reached a relatively peaceful time as our nest slowly empties. She needs her space, and my mother does not know the meaning of the word. Yet, what about what I owe my mother? Can I leave her in her helplessness and not fulfill the role that seems to have landed on my shoulders? Is this the example I want to set for my children? Part of me almost wishes for my wife to refuse; then I can get rid of this awful guilt because I can tell myself that I tried. How many fragments can one heart hold?

Well, my wife has been asking for communication for years. I somehow don't think this is exactly what she envisioned, but I think the time has come for me to share my sentiments and even ask her if perhaps she could find it in her heart to invite my mother to live with us. I know it will be hard, but maybe with her new, more understanding husband, we can navigate this together.

"Umm, honey, can we talk?"

Section Two: Allies and Alibies

Fired!

APRIL SPEAKS / DIRECTOR KAREN SPEAKS

April Speaks:

Straightening my shoulders, I smooth my hair as I walk towards the administrator's office. It's just a meeting about next year, I soothe my anxious nerves, nothing to get all worked up about. They'll mention how much I've added to the office ambience, how much the patients appreciate my warm, personal touch, and hey, maybe they'll even offer me a raise. And I'll smile modestly, inwardly agreeing that I, young though I may be, surely am more computer savvy than all of them combined.

"We don't know how we managed before you came on board, April," the administrator will tell me, shaking her head with an admiring smile on her lips. "So we'd like to invite you..."

That will be the perfect segue into my rejoinder. The only question is whether I should accept their offer of a contract renewal, or if I should come straight with them. Although I enjoy the challenge of working in this happening office- Dr. Hirsch is a renowned dermatologist, and people wait months to get an appointment with him- there's a long commute involved that's difficult to handle, especially now that I have to factor in the baby. So if I would agree to stay on, it would have to be with the stipulation of an increase in salary.

Knocking on Director Karen Fine's door, she calls "Come in," and I enter her office.

"Make yourself comfortable," she says, and I slide into a seat on the other side of her desk.

"How is it going for you this year?" she asks me in a friendly tone, folding her hands neatly on top of her cluttered desk. *After we get through with the technicalities, maybe I'll offer to help her get organized.*

"I'm happy here," I reply. "I've updated our files, switched to a more efficient communication mode, and really enjoy the patient interaction."

Okay, Karen, now it's time to make me an offer I can't refuse. To show how much you appreciate my dedication, my willingness to sometimes stay late or to fill in for someone last minute...

She hesitates. "I don't know how to say this, April. This is hard for me, too. Your work is excellent, and we really enjoy having you on staff. But due to some recent cutbacks, we're being forced to downsize. And sadly, the only logical place to start is with staff that has come on board more recently, irrespective of their stellar performance."

Huh? Didn't she read the script? Why do I feel like the rug was just pulled out from under me? I'm sinking. I will absolutely not cry in front of her. No way! But I do think I've been- fired?

"So I thank you for your wonderful year of service, but we won't be renewing your contract. I trust you'll find something well suited to your multi-faceted talents."

"I understand," I say, nodding and pasting a thin smile on my lips while my insides implode in strident protest. "I wish you all the best."

I walk out standing tall, grateful that they don't have x-ray vision to see my inner turmoil. *I've just been fired! Those total and complete incompetent fools just fired me! ME, April Green, graduate of Gold Computer Technologies. Of all the nerve! How dare they! Are they nuts? Don't they know I was head and shoulders above my classmates? How will they ever replace me? That's the thanks I get for putting in overtime without a word of protest?*

Granted, I was debating about resigning anyway. But that would have been okay- it would have been my decision, and I would have felt so validated when they fell to their knees and begged me to stay on. But whoa, it hurts to be rejected. Being fired feels like part of my essence has been trampled. I know it's really for the good; I know I'll find something better. But my self-esteem has suffered a blow, and for now, it really hurts. Fired? Me?

Director Karen Speaks:

I don't know if most people dream of becoming a human resource director. If we took polls of elementary age children, there would be many more aspiring teachers, firemen, doctors, and policemen. Yet I always was a non-conformist. Growing up in a very poor home and watching a widowed mother struggle to support her children, the seed of yearning to help people find jobs found a home in my heart. What a joyful profession, I daydreamed, to pair the ideal candidate with the job best suited to his or her talents and abilities. What could be more satisfying than helping someone earn a respectable living and feel the satisfaction of being productive?

Focused on this lofty mission from the age of 12, I took extra courses while still in high school, and asked as many adults who gave me time and attention about how they found their jobs. I even dared to ask if they felt happy doing what they were doing for so many of their waking hours- a significant part of their lives. Much to my idealistic distress, many said no, that they lived for vacation. I was horrified and determined to change the world. People spend years of their lives at work. I, Karen, could not sit back and allow this dismal state of affairs to continue. Even as a student, my friends and I could identify the teachers who felt a passion for transmitting knowledge in striking contrast to those who appeared to just be doing a job. And those classes dragged by very slowly. Usually there were far more discipline issues, as well. Did I behave, you wonder? Well, some things must remain confidential.

Fast forward to my current position. I love the satisfaction of matching people to their ideal jobs. I love the sparkle of excitement when people learn that they are hired for the position of their dreams. However, there is one aspect of my position that I would love to delegate or delete from my job description. When a company needs to downsize, and the time comes to tell an employee that for various reasons her job will be terminated, there is no easy way to perform this surgery. Just knowing that the employee will experience rejection and betrayal, and that I am the source of that is the opposite of my dreams, it becomes more like my worst nightmare. Often, an employee enters the office dreaming of receiving raises and accolades for a job well done, only to hear that the contract will not be renewed.

Just recently, I had to fire an employee by the name of April Green. She walked confidently into my office with every reason to feel proud of her achievements. However, in the current economic climate, our business has the opportunity to save a significant amount of money by downsizing the amount of our staff members. April truly deserves an increase in salary, not to mention a transportation allowance for her commute. Yet I sense a growing dissatisfaction in her, as her intelligence far exceeds the nature of the work we can offer her.

I know April, with her advanced skill set, will probably find something more suited to her talents and capabilities. Our decision makes sense on many levels, and yet it seems so unfair to cause pain to an employee who truly fulfilled every requirement for her job description and even made improvements in the efficiency of the office. At the same time, she is the newest employee, and we do have to show loyalty to our long-term employees. No one ever warned me about the hurtful aspect of human resource services...

April is a truly a talented and remarkable young woman. She does not belong here- she is capable of so much more. I know the time will come when she will thank me. Sometimes people remain in a safe environment, not venturing beyond because of fear of the unknown. I gave her a push, which may hurt in the moment, but will likely become a source of ever growing momentum as she seeks to utilize her unique skills and earns a salary more commensurate with her education. If she only knew that underneath my confident and firm exterior, her shock and dismay touch me deeply and make me question my own fit for this position.

Maybe I can write her a note expressing my willingness to write a warm letter of recommendation. In fact, I will do that right now.

"Dear April,

It would be my pleasure to write you a note of recommendation. Please let me know if this will be helpful. Thank you for your wonderful service. We will miss having you here. "

Oh Look!

KARLY SPEAKS / STUEY SPEAKS

Karly Speaks:

Oh look, a new letter from South Africa! I wonder how Stuey and Susan are enjoying the beautiful summer weather- we have three feet of snow covering the ground.

Every time we get a letter, it reminds me of my pivotal date with Jack. Hard to believe it's been twenty years already...

"So tell me more about what it was really like growing up in South Africa. It must have been such a culture shock traveling overseas to school and leaving your family so far away. "

"I will admit to being homesick, and the guys good-naturedly imitated my accent all the time. But, you will love my family and they really want to meet you. Am I getting ahead of myself over here, Karly?"

Hearing my name on his lips sent goosebumps up and down my flesh. And sure enough, within the month, he proposed and we were officially bride and groom. And, oh, the excitement that began to fill my heart- this was really happening.

Having grown up in a very small family, I longed for the sense of belonging to a larger whole. If Jack's family was anything like him, I could look forward to a whole new family ready to welcome me with open arms. I am so grateful for such an amazing guy and for realizing my dream of a larger dynamic family to share.

Yet, life has a way of leading us in unexpected directions. Five years after our marriage, we received a magnificent invitation to my brother-in-law's high school graduation.

"Jack, can you believe your brother is graduating next month? I am so excited to go to South Africa and see the family again. It's been quite a while."

"Umm, Karly..."

"Yes, Jack, this is so exciting! I need to shop. Do you think I should wear my black dress or get a new dress for the occasion?"

"Karly-"

"Yes, Jack. I definitely need new shoes, and you need a suit. We need to make your family proud."

"Karly, there is something I need to discuss with you."

"Oh, sure, Jack, any time, always happy to hear what you have to say. Why don't we first just finish this South Africa shopping list and then I'll be all ears?"

"Karly, what I need to discuss pertains directly to South Africa."

"Oh, Jack, why didn't you say so? Don't tell me your brother sent extra funding to handle these expenses! You know, maybe that's just too much for us to accept."

"Karly, I really need to talk with you."

"Oh, Jack, I enjoy our talks too. Can you believe it has been five years since we've been there? Can I make you a coffee?"

"Karly, this is very hard for me to explain. I know how excited you've been to go back to South Africa and see the family. But my brother's funding is a bit dry at the moment- I'm sorry, Karly- he only sent a ticket for me."

My jaw dropped open. Trying to conceal the pain, disappointment and even the sense of betrayal that my husband would willingly go without me, I swallowed the growing lump in my throat.

"Oh, well I guess, I will just toss this list then. You go, have a great time, and give everyone my best. Tickets are expensive. I understand."

This pattern repeated itself every couple of years for varied occasions. One ticket would arrive in the mail, and Jack would fly away to that magnificent country to enjoy quality time with his family while I stayed home nursing disappointment and trying to cleanse myself from the hurt. Aren't I part of the family, too?

Why do they just want Jack?

Yet, always wanting to be the good wife, I summoned a tremulous smile and packed him off with lots of food and warm wishes to enjoy while the kids and I counted the days till his return.

Fast-forward twenty years. My brother-in-law was preparing a huge bash in South Africa for my in-laws' fiftieth anniversary. Mentally preparing myself for that familiar feeling of self-pity and exclusion, plus a gold star award for martyrdom, I opened the by now familiar South African stamped letter.

Dear Jack and Karly,

Enclosed are two tickets for you and Karly to join us at the upcoming anniversary party. Can't wait to see you there.

Love,

Your dear brother

Ecstatic, I waved the letter in front of Jack's eyes.

"Jack, Jack, can we talk?"

"Karly, haven't we had these talks for so many years? I thought you understand my need to see my family and our own limited budget."

"Jack, Jack-

"Yes, Karly, I know it's hard for you. I wish it could be different."

"Jack, please listen!"

"Karly, I can repeat each of our parts in this conversation in my sleep. Maybe we should take each other's lines for some variety."

I stuck the letter under his nose and pulled out the two tickets with shining eyes.

"I guess, this means we're official now. Which dress should I wear to the anniversary party?"

Stuey Speaks:

"Karen, we need to talk about the graduation." I turned to my wife with a smile, excited to plan our first real milestone event together.

"I know. I can't believe it's coming up so soon. Just three more months and so much to do! I have to outfit all the kids, talk to the caterer and the photographer..."

"Yep, all those things need to be taken care of. No one said making a family celebration is easy. But I was thinking about something else. Do you know it's been five years since I last saw my brother, Jack? I'd really like to send him a ticket. He's my only brother and he should be with us for a family occasion."

"That's really generous of you, Stuey. Especially now when things are a little tight."

"Well, I know he can't afford to come unless we bring him in. I wish we could send one for Karly, too, but I just don't see how we can. Between all the expenses that keep cropping up, two tickets would put us over the top. But I think we can handle one."

"So do it!" Susan said, "It will be so nice for the two of you to have some time together. I'm sure Karly will understand."

•••

A few years and another milestone later...

"Congratulations!" Susan beamed as she called family and friends with the amazing news. Diane was engaged!

A few nights later, once the initial excitement had ebbed a bit, my wife and I sat on the couch talking over cups of hot tea.

"You know, Susan, here we go again. This is feeling like déjà vu. I really want to send Jack a ticket for the wedding. Do we have the extra money? Not really. We have two children in college, plus all the wedding expenses. Invitations, gowns, suits, hall, caterer, kitchen stuff and linens...is there an end? Our business is doing okay, but there's a limit. I think we have to cut where we can. So I guess I'll send one ticket again. I wish we could bring them both in, but..."

"You can only do what you can do," Susan murmured, sipping her cinnamon tea. "We're not made of money, you know. And we are making a wedding. They'll just have to understand."

I hoped they really did understand. I wonder how I would feel if the tables were turned. Was Karly really okay with this situation, or were there unknown blisters festering? Shaking my head, I decided not to dwell on it. It's not like we could change the situation anyway.

With each occasion the same scenario replayed.

Fast-forward twenty years...

"We should really do something for Mom and Dad's fiftieth. What do you think?" As I turned to my wife and life partner, I knew she would be happy to create a memorable celebration for our parents.

"You're right, Stuey. Such a special occasion calls for something big," Susan agreed.

"You know, I've been thinking. Our kids are all out of college, and our years of support are long over. Plus I got a special bonus this month. We just picked up two new clients, and they're big ones. So this time, I think we can afford to bring in Jack and Karly together. Won't that be nice?"

Susan breathed a sigh of relief. Well, if there really had been hard feelings over the years, maybe this would help them dissipate.

"Now that will be a real celebration. The whole family together!"

And the Winner Is...

PRINCIPAL SPEAKS / MRS. STAMPS SPEAKS

Principal Speaks:

"Good morning, everyone, and welcome." I allow my eyes to rove the room, taking a few moments to acknowledge everyone in attendance. "I'm excited to present a new idea for our students. We will be having a school-wide competition in basic Mathematics. The students will have a month to prepare..."

"A school-wide competition?" Mrs. Stamps, a loyal and long-time teacher, interrupts, her tone sharp and cutting. "How can you do that? Do you realize what you will do to their self-esteem? I thought our school prides itself on utilizing *proper* educational methods."

Her tirade continued, and it took all of my strength to keep my face neutral and my lips clamped. How could she do this? Yell at the principal publicly, disagreeing so vehemently in front of my faculty?

Calling a fifteen-minute recess from our meeting, I step into my office for a few minutes to decompress. *What just happened?* I wondered, putting my head down on my desk as a sudden rush of fatigue overpowered me. Did Mrs. Stamps really just explode like a volcano when I broached the idea of a school-wide competition?

Is this cause for termination? My thoughts swirl in cyclonic upheaval, and I take a few deep breaths to stay my pounding heart. If she can lose control so quickly and easily, perhaps she can no longer be entrusted to nurture and mold the souls of our sweet, innocent third graders. It is my job, first and foremost, to consider the educational needs of our children. Perhaps Mrs. Stamps is ready for retirement and has lost what it takes to be in the classroom. In fact, maybe it's a positive twist that this first episode happened at a staff meeting and not in her classroom. This way we can handle it before any of our children are hurt. Not to mention the fact that she publicly berated me in front of the entire faculty. However, as a professional, I would never allow personal feelings to get in the way of fulfilling my responsibilities. The real question is: Does Mrs. Stamps serve as a role model and educator for our children and staff? After this volatile outburst, I fear the answer may be no...

Come to think of it, I do wonder what triggered her reaction. During the decade that Mrs. Stamps served as part of our faculty, she never conducted herself in the manner she displayed today. In fact, her students seem to genuinely like her, and their learning is on target with the curriculum. She encourages them when they're hesitant and praises their efforts. This was a strange deviation. Hmmm... could it be that she once had a terrible experience from competition and that's why she feels so strongly? And even more, maybe she's trying to protect her students from suffering the pain that she experienced? That does put a different spin on things.

I will have to explain to her the benefits of competition, and maybe she'll change her view. That is, if she's calm when we reconvene. I think I might take an Advil before going back.

Okay, Mrs. Principal, since practice makes perfect, imagine Mrs. Stamps is right here in front of you. How would you endorse competition so she can see your point?

Mrs. Stamps, thank you in advance for hearing me out. Competition can be a real learning experience for children, helping to prepare them for the real world. Isn't that the essence of education? When they leave the safety of our secure haven there will be college and careers around the bend. Their performances will be evaluated, and their levels of success may gain them status or financial remuneration. It's not healthy to shield our children from what life will bring their way. We want them to have coping skills and be confident when confronted by life's challenges.

Yes, she'll surely see my point when I present it so logically. As far as her job, since this was a one-time aberration, I think I can overlook it this time, although I certainly hope she apologizes. But if it ever happens again...

Mrs. Stamps Speaks:

Is it true that I, a veteran teacher, lost total control at the recent staff meeting? When the principal innocently brought up the words "school wide competition", my blood began to boil and the words poured out almost involuntarily. It is a matter of principle, right? Doesn't everyone have areas about which they are very passionate, especially when there could be potential harm to vulnerable children? The other staff members will need to think more carefully before nodding in acquiescence at every new project that may bring PR to the school without a careful evaluation of the consequences. So, we may have state winners and get extra funding, but at what cost?

I took a deep breath and tried to calm myself. *Look in the mirror, dear teacher. Passion about ideas does not usually yield emotional explosions and a total resistance to hearing any dissenting opinions. What happened to listening to other ideas and considering their merits? Flexibility? Negotiation? Win-win solutions? Modeling the behavior we want to teach? Out of the window in your fit of rage...*

This was not a normal response from me. What's really going on? I decided to open the window within and take a deep breath.

I could picture the day in my mind, even though getting the salutatorian award instead of being the valedictorian happened over thirty years ago. That wound cannot still be festering, or can it? And then when my kids were young, it hurt when I was not invited to the honor roll breakfasts. My children were not wired to be angelic students. Yet, somehow I internalized this as my parental failure. Furthermore, how many graduations did I attend when most of the parents and students cringed and just a select few, as determined by the staff, merited to be publicly acknowledged? Oh, there is so much personal pain here. I have to acknowledge it honestly. Only then can I deal with it rather than suppress it and pretend it will go away. Yes, I wonder how much experience shapes my opinions as opposed to just intellectual research.

Research can generally go both ways. I am unapologetic for my stance, yet filled with remorse for my outburst; I need to return to the staffroom for a real conversation where we can explore the benefits and the risks to competition in school, emotions aside.

A Little 'Cell-f' Reflection

LIBBY SPEAKS / CASHIER SPEAKS

Libby Speaks:

Just look around- no one talks to each other anymore. Bent over their devices, everyone is engrossed in their own world, which in our technologically advanced society, doesn't even cause concern anymore. Back when I was growing up, carrying on a one-sided conversation could result in a knowing glance followed by an urgent summons to the men in white coats.

I believe in personal communication, and unlike this modern decadent society, model cell phone etiquette at its best. For example, my gym had to come up with a policy forbidding cell phones during class. Can you believe that was necessary? In the middle of aerobics and weight training, countless participants think nothing of walking off to chat on their phones, much to the teacher's incredulity and raised eyebrows (does raising eyebrows burn more calories? Maybe I'll try it). And how about in stores, when customers don't wish the cashier a good day because they are otherwise occupied in seemingly more significant conversations? Okay, time to get off my soapbox.

Oh, my cell phone is ringing. I'd better check to see if it's important. "Hi, Sandy, how are you?" It's my only sister calling all the way from Mexico City! Because of the time difference, we often have trouble reaching each other. "Great, just walking into a store, so don't mind if I try to keep my voice on the low end. You have something important to tell me? Okay, I'm all ears. David is proposing tonight? WOW! My cute, little nephew- Double wow! I want to hear all the details...Tell me. That's amazing- I'm so happy for you!

As we talked, I became aware of a hurt expression on the face of a dear friend who walked by me with her shopping cart. I nodded at her as she passed, but I was deeply engrossed in my sister's news. Surely she can't be annoyed with me! I'm finally talking with my only sister, and this is vitally important. If she knew the background, she would understand.

I continue listening to everything about this paragon of a fiancé from the time she was in preschool.

Just as I was enjoying this detailed rendition, this friend walked by me once again and looked like she wanted to say something, shook her head sadly and walked away. Now, my conscience was activated. Did I unwittingly hurt her?

I said goodbye to Sandy, now hyper focused on the sad expression on my friend's face and feeling very guilty. Sometimes, no matter what we do, guilt has a way of worming its way into our heads and making itself feel quite at home. Should I not have given Sandy my full attention? Should I have promised to call her back in order to greet my friend? Should I have explained to my friend about the nature of the chat even though they were not officially engaged yet and it was really not her business? No, that's a no brainer. That was confidential and not my information to share.

Oh well, more dilemmas to ponder which will hopefully just allow me to grow.

Cashier Speaks:

What a long journey from teaching in a classroom to working as a cashier. Logically, I understand that we moved late in the summer and the teaching jobs were taken already. Yet my heart feels so disappointed. What a difference when there is a passion and purpose in your work and lives can be transformed by a special relationship. I guess working as a cashier can help me become more humble. When someone I recognize observes me doing this job, I feel like crawling into a shell and hiding, unlike my experience as a teacher. Knowing that I was a link in transmitting knowledge to the next generation filled me with pride and self-respect. I stood up straight even during the most challenging of times. That thought deserves more reflection, as our jobs do not define us or determine our worth. But once again, that's logic speaking, which is a long distance away from my emotional reality.

But this time belongs to Tasty Tidbits as the next customer approaches my station. Maybe some solution focused therapeutic strategies that I used to implement in my classroom can help me here and now.

This is my current situation and it makes sense to accept it and make the best of it. And so, I will talk myself through this and hopefully arrive in a better place.

Transforming lives can be done in any environment as it's about the warmth and care that I exude.

Identify the aspects that I loved about my job and see how many can be applied here.

Working with people, opportunities for personal growth, learning, and teaching.

Forming connections and relationships, helping others, encouraging people.

Wait one minute. There is not one item on this list that cannot be worked on even from a cashier station. Here comes from my first opportunity.

Cashier: Good morning. I hope you found everything you needed.

Customer: Plastic bags, those large zip lock bags work really well.

Cashier: I'm glad you found them helpful.

Customer: Yes, my new hat traveled without getting messed up at all.

Cashier: Sorry, were you looking for a certain size bag? Aisle 4 has all of our bags of many assorted sizes.

Customer: You are so right. It is absolutely inspirational. I can't wait to tell people about this!

Cashier: Thank you. No one has ever been so gracious just to receive a bit of guidance.

Customer: Yes, awesome! Kiwis and pineapples would add a very colorful and healthy touch. Do you think you can help with that?

Cashier: My pleasure, the fruit is in aisle 2 and we got a beautiful shipment of kiwis in just today.

Customer: Absolutely, I know you are incredibly helpful. They hit the jackpot with hiring you.

Cashier: Thank you, that is so nice of you to say. This is a new job and I am so pleased to be able to help you.

Customer: One second, Halley. Oh, excuse me were you speaking to me? I am on the phone with a very close friend. Just please add up my purchases and let me know what I owe you. Okay, Halley what were you saying?

Cashier: Have a nice day,

Customer: Bye, Halley, talk to you later. Oh, were you talking to me again? Yes, sure, you too, thanks.

I cannot become discouraged just because one person was multitasking and combining her shopping time with her social time. People are very busy. Although it was mortifying when I thought she was complimenting me, I can't believe I didn't see her headset. In fact, I was having a monologue, thinking we were communicating. I can certainly understand a busy person's need to have some social time. However, if she took a quick breath from her conversation long enough to notice and acknowledge my presence, it would certainly have been polite.

Maybe this is part of what I am supposed to learn in this field of work beyond trying to do mental math in a way that would make my fourth grade teacher beam with pride. And the good news is that there can be some real opportunities to help even in a job like this. And I am sure that there will be many opportunities to help people in a variety of ways.

Here comes Libby. I have a lot of respect for her.

Cashier: Hello, Libby. Did you find everything okay?

Libby: well, I am a bit distracted and have a feeling that this may be one of those shopping trips where I bring home everything except what I came here to buy.

Cashier: That happens to all of us at times. Is there something specific that I can help you locate?

Libby: That is very kind of you. This work must be an adjustment for you. You seem to have teacher written all over you.

Cashier: That is very kind of you to say. I am experiencing some adjustment pains. I hope the distraction you mentioned is only about your involvement in many wonderful projects.

Libby: I feel badly because while I was speaking on the cell in your store, something I ordinarily don't do, I apparently offended a close friend in the process.

Of course I apologized, yet here I was enjoying a special conversation with my sister and unwittingly caused someone else discomfort.

Cashier: Libby, it sounds like you usually take great pains to be respectful of people.

Libby: It's so interesting because I see this prevalent cell phone use as negative and impeding connections between people. Yet when I received a special call, I picked it up enthusiastically and those sensitivities went out the window.

Cashier: It sounds like a human reaction when receiving a call from someone close to us. What is bothering you the most about what happened?

Libby: Since there is no one behind me in line, we can talk. I truly want to be a considerate person and I do want people to think positively of me. And not only did I fail in this instance, I judged others who do the same thing as rude.

Cashier: I see, so it is far more than the cell phone, isn't it?

Libby: Yes, the cell phone just triggered this thought process.

Cashier: Libby, I can see this is really making you upset. You are clearly a person who tries to be one with her values. And, on the rare occasion that you make a mistake, it is really hard for you.

Libby: Exactly. I don't really give myself permission to make mistakes, especially not embarrassing ones in public.

Cashier: I hear you. I am curious if these very high standards create hardships for you in other areas also?

Libby: Have you been watching through my window lately? There is so much tension from feeling that I am walking on eggshells, always afraid that I may crack one.

Cashier: That sounds so painful- like the smile on your face can be wiped away any time there is the slightest mistake.

Libby: Do you mean like with the cell phone? Well, you have to admit that was pretty terrible.

Cashier: Look, I can tell you that as a cashier, it is very unpleasant and often embarrassing when people continue with their conversations as if I don't exist. But a person who answers an occasional call- is she doing something terrible? The bigger question is- are we allowed to make mistakes, do our best to repair them, and move forward with a smile?

Libby: Are you suggesting that I be a little more tolerant towards myself?

Cashier: I could not have said it any better.

Libby: Well, you certainly gave me more than I what I shopped for. By the way, have you ever considered coaching?

Passing the Buck

BETTY SPEAKS / RHODA SPEAKS

Betty Speaks:

T'was the week before our yearly family reunion, and as I was cooking and baking up a storm, I found myself dreaming of sitting on my rocking chair sipping coffee and enjoying some leisure time. Burrowed inside my kitchen cabinets, the doorbell jarred me from my undignified position.

"Hi, Sally, how are you?" I greeted my friend standing at my door, anxious to be back in the kitchen.

"So-so," she said quietly. "May I come in?"

Did I have a choice? Her eyes looked a bit misty, and I wondered what she needed. And with a sudden epiphany, I knew.

Sally's husband had been unemployed for the last year, and she had been flitting from job to job, desperately trying to support their family singlehandedly. Just looking at her face made me sure that her best efforts were inadequate and that she was approaching her friends in search of help. My thoughts were traveling like a high-speed train racing down the tracks, and I knew what I had to do. Better to let her know right away so she would know to look elsewhere.

"We can't pay our electric bill," Sally was saying, wiping her eyes. "I don't know what to do. And my landlord is threatening us with eviction."

That's really bad, I thought. I don't know anyone who could just open their doors to a family of five without blinking an eye.

"Can I get you a drink?" I offered, my eyes radiating sympathy.

"No. I can't drink. I can't eat. I need five hundred dollars by tomorrow," she pleaded. "Between that and my check, I should be able to handle this month's rent. Can you help me?"

"Sally," I explained softly, "I'm in charge of a charity fund that helps families with medical needs. The fund that I have can only be used for those types of situations. I'm so sorry…"

"You don't understand," she interrupted. "I'm asking you. Personally. I'm desperate. Please, Betty…"

Me? Us? The family who is always in the red? Is she joking? How I wish…

"Let me call my husband," I demurred, grabbing the phone and racing into a back room. I knew what he would say, but didn't know what else to do.

"We can give her twenty-five," my husband offered. "I wish we had more, but we just don't."

"I wish we could do more, Sally," I explained, handing her the meager sum. "But I'm going to work on this. I walked Sally to the door, and the pain of her situation washed over me. Taking in her sagging shoulders and woebegone expression, I determined to raise the money. As soon as she left, I got on the phone. One of my first calls was to Rhoda, the person in charge of our communal charity fund. I poured the story into her listening ears.

"Betty," Rhoda said, "Helping Hands has done all we can for Sally's family at this point. We've given and given, and simply don't have any more to pour into their family situation. I feel terrible, but there are other community needs as well."

My heart dropped into my stomach. Strike one. I leafed through our directory and began calling doctors' wives. Miraculously, pledges began coming in.

"Who do I make the check out to?" they asked me. "We want it to be tax deductible."

"Oh, to Helping Hands would be fine," I answered quickly, knowing that since they were a larger and more established fund than the one I was in charge of, sometimes people preferred to donate to their account. I figured Helping Hands would then be happy to write a check from their account for Sally's family, and everyone would be happy.

By the end of the next day, I collected not five but six hundred dollars in pledges! I felt accomplished and humbled at the same time, and almost incredulous that I had succeeded. Unfortunately, I didn't have all the money in hand by Sally's deadline, and I nervously dialed her number.

"Don't worry," Sally reassured me. "My son just paid our rent. With your help, I'll be able to pay the electric bill so they don't turn off our power. I can collect it on Sunday."

I breathed a sigh of relief and resumed my preparations. Until the phone rang.

"Betty?"

"Oh, hi, Rhoda."

"Did you tell the Campbells to make out their check to Helping Hands, and then we would hand you a check for Sally's family?"

"Yes," I answered.

"How could you do that?"

Huh?

"I told you we can't do any more for their family! How could you take that liberty without speaking to me? That is totally unacceptable."

"I- I'm sorry. I thought you couldn't help them directly from your fund. But I didn't know you would have a problem filtering the money if it came from outside sources. I've asked you to do that at other times- have you forgotten- and never had an issue."

"Well it's a big issue, and you've made it very sticky for me. I don't know what to do now."

"I'll just tell the Campbells to write their check to my fund. I'm sorry for the trouble."

Shaking, I hung up the phone and blinked back some tears. I felt somewhat dazed, unsure why I had just received that stinging slap. Here I had left my comfort zone to help a poverty stricken family at an insanely busy time, and I get yelled at? By the head of a charity committee, no less! How could she speak to me like that?

I took a few minutes to compose myself, and then I picked up the phone. I didn't want to bear a grudge, so I knew what I had to do.

"Rhoda," I began, "I need to share something with you. All I did was try to help Sally's family because they are desperate. I don't really understand why you got so upset. As I said, I've handled charitable donations like that, with your consent and assistance, in the past and certainly meant no harm. I don't want to continue feeling hurt and angry, so I figured we could try to talk this through."

"I'm sorry," Rhoda conceded, although her tone didn't sound conciliatory. "I didn't mean to hurt you. But I thought you understood the situation from our first conversation."

"If I understood," I countered, "then why would I have gone ahead and done this? After all these years, don't you know me a little better than that?"

"I'm sorry," she repeated, sounding more sincere this time.

"Okay," I sniffed. "If the heads of charitable organizations can't get along, we're in trouble." I waited to hear a chuckle, but there was silence. Oh, well. "Take care of yourself."

"You, too," she said.

Hurt feelings continued to linger, and I struggled to find the message. I had tried so hard to help Sally- why was I beset by this pain?

When Sally came on Sunday, she couldn't thank me enough. Her effusive appreciation soothed my wound.

"I'm so glad you came to me," I told her. "And I'm grateful I was able to help. Good luck to you!"

She gave me a warm hug and ran off with the envelope in hand.

Time has passed, and whenever I see Rhoda, I smile warmly. But I can still taste the bitterness of that encounter...

Rhoda Speaks:

Okay, Rhoda, it's time to start with those affirmations the life coach recommended during your last session. Remember, the test of real learning is by application.

Being responsible for communal funds is a pressure, burden and one of the most stressful jobs I have ever accepted.

Come on, Rhoda, you can do better than that. You practiced very well during the executive coaching session. Dr. L, the master coach par excellence, actually chose you to give a demo for the rest of the group. I know my words were a cover-up, but I have always been a skilled actress. Okay here goes take two:

Being responsible for communal funds is a privilege. Much better, now let's say it again as though you really mean and feel it. Breathe in the privilege of helping others experiencing financial hardship. Exhale the toxicity of people whipping the messenger. Inhale the kindness and appreciation; exhale the anger at the irresponsible "do gooders" who endanger our bookkeeping with their golden hearts and utter cluelessness at how the system needs to operate to remain viable. One final deep, cleansing breath, and stretch...

Oh, there's the phone. Calmness pervades every cell in my mind and body. "Why, hello Betty. How are you? It's lovely to hear from you. How can I help you?

"You would like to help Sally? Betty, here is the problem. We only have a certain amount of resources, which need to be fairly allocated to each and every genuine need as determined by a board of carefully selected individuals that oversee our charity work. As much as Sally's situation seems heart wrenching, she has already received as much as we can justify giving her without taking away from other families that also deserve our help and also find themselves in exceedingly challenging situations.

"Thanks for your understanding, and I wish it could be different."

Why do I have this uncomfortable feeling that Betty, sensitive soul that she is, was not focused on the content of our conversation? It sounded like Sally's plight really saddened her. She would not take our procedures and change anything on her own, right? I do not need to worry, since I was very clear with her. Why do I feel that niggling feeling in my stomach?

There goes the phone again. It's our bookkeeper. I am proud to say that all of our accounts are accurate and in keeping with the policies that our board of directors formulated. "Hello. Yes, this is Rhoda. There is a problem with Sally's account. I know for a fact that we did not exceed the recommended amount for a family of her size with her financial constraints. We will have to pay a fine now due to this oversight. Can you please show me the offensive paper work because something is wrong with this picture? We work so industriously to ensure that we have dotted every i and crossed every t to guarantee total transparency and follow through with an organization of this nature.

"Someone sent a check with funds earmarked for Sally. Why would anyone do that without consulting me? It could not have been Betty. I will just call and check. I am sure she would not do that right after I explained the nature of our restrictions. Although she was so caught up in Sally's plight, there is only one way to find out."

It was Betty. I will work on forgiving her, but I will have to be firm and assertive this time because our organization cannot afford to waste money on fines for breaking procedural policies. As much as she spearheads her medical assistance fund, she does not have any special privileges with the funds of Helping Hands. I have to let her know that in this case a yes to Sally means a no to another needy individual.

"Hello Betty, you did not, by any chance, ear mark funds for Sally after we spoke, did you? You did???

"Betty, we are having major challenges with the bookkeeper now that you chose to follow your heart. And I am disturbed that you would choose to do this despite our earlier conversation.

"I work very hard and even need special coaching so as not to send my blood pressure through the roof. I certainly do not appreciate when you take our carefully designed system and toss it out in the garbage.

"Okay, as long as you know for next time. Have a great day."

Later, Betty called again saying that she was hurt? I am scratching my head in utter befuddlement.

Affirmation time again. Go ahead, Rhoda, let's show Dr. L. that yours truly applied her recommendations during highly stressful moments.

Being responsible for communal funds is a pressure, burden, and one of the most stressful jobs I have ever accepted...

A Telling Moment

KARLA SPEAKS / RONNIE SPEAKS

Karla Speaks:

Busy having a blast in high school, I had important things on my agenda, like reveling in my large part in our upcoming play, maintaining my high A average, and keeping up with my friends, which was a job in itself. Endowed with a naturally outgoing, extroverted personality, I thrived on social interaction- lots of it. It nourished my soul much like my three meals a day sustained my body. Yet over the past few months, I had been feeling distinctly unwell. Slightly nauseous with some recurrent abdominal pain, I kept putting it on the back burner- who had time to be sick? And why worry my mother when it was probably just a call for extra rest and less stress? But when my symptoms began to get worse and I could no longer hide the way I was feeling, my mother's antennae began twitching, and off we went to our family practitioner. Dr. R took copious notes, examined me, and when the results of the blood work came in a few days later, so did his unwelcome call.

"Take her to the hospital," he told my mother, "Immediately."

When my mother picked me up early from school and delivered her bombshell, my world imploded.

"Now?" I squeaked, "But I have play practice today!"

"Karla, I'm so sorry," she said, squeezing my hand reassuringly. "I know how hard this is. But we may be dealing with something that needs medical attention, and if we don't get it under control, it can get worse- quickly. We have no choice."

I glanced at my mother, whose face looked white, and my heart dropped. *The hospital? Me? Was I dreaming? And what exactly were they afraid I had?* Terrified, I was afraid to ask. *Maybe if I didn't ask, it wouldn't become reality...*

Several days later we had our diagnosis: Crohn's disease.

"Hopefully the medication will manage it, and you can continue with your regular lifestyle and activities," the nurse assured me as she signed my discharge papers.

Hopefully? The dubious word dangled tenuously in my mind as I made a sudden dash for the bathroom. My mother's consternation was thick and tangible, and I could feel her eyes boring into my back before I slammed the door.

•••

Thankfully, years have passed since my initial diagnosis, and my Crohn's has been eminently manageable. That memorable hospitalization was my only one. Sure, I had the occasional flare up that required some consultation and medical intervention. Switching medications or a new dose consistently remedied the problem, and no one was able to look at me and see a girl with a serious condition. I kept up with the best of 'em. I attended a prestigious college, and returned all fired up, ready to embark on the next new and exciting stage of my life: the job market. To my surprise, a few weeks after landing a job as a medical assistant, a young, handsome PA asked me out for a date.

Months passed, and I was feeling closer and closer to Ronny. What a great guy! Could he be The One? I knew he was getting serious, too. But there was one thing that interfered with my happiness, like a neon light that kept flashing in my mind. Should I tell him about my illness? The worry about his reaction kept me up nights. What if he drops me?

Maybe he would have even refused to go out with me had he known about my situation, I worried.

Applying my make-up, I peered into the mirror once more as the doorbell rang. Ronny was here for me. I couldn't help but wonder how I would feel if someone had concealed such vital information from me. Honest self-reflection told me I would be furious, feeling deceived and betrayed. *Will he drop me? Will anyone want me? Don't cry,* I ordered myself as I slowly descended the stairs. *It will ruin your make-up.*

Ronny Speaks:

"Yes, Dad, I really like Karla. I felt comfortable with her from the very first date, and we seem to have common interests and goals. Our conversations flow so naturally, and I enjoy listening to her comments and questions. At the end of each date, I leave feeling that we had not run short of topics to discuss."

"It sounds like you did not come with any question, Ronny. Everything sounds great!"

My father's encouragement boosted my excitement, and I continued seeing Karla, daring to dream as our relationship deepened.

Each of our dates was enjoyable, and I could only see wonderful traits in Karla.

"Thank you, Karla, for a very nice evening."

"Before we call it a night, I have something I need to tell you." She looked nervous.

"Sure, I'd be happy to hear what's on your mind."

"This is not easy for me to say. When I was in high school, I was diagnosed with Crohn's disease. It was a shock to all of us, and thank G-d, has been well under control ever since I learned how to manage it. I eat very nutritiously and prioritize regular exercise. Please understand that it was not our intention to deceive you by waiting until now to inform you. I understand that you will need time to think."

"This discovery must have really shaken you up and been a very difficult challenge."

"I am sorry. I didn't mean to start crying." She quickly brushed away the tears.

"Did I say something wrong? Sorry, if I upset you."

"No, you responded so empathetically. I'm just relieved."

"Oh, my mother does that sometimes, too. You thought I might get angry and walk away in a cloud of thunder. I have not done that since I was nine. At that age, my tantrums could be heard from across the street. Remind me later to tell you that story."

"But," I saw Karla tense up as I continued, "you realize I will have to do some serious thinking about where this puts our relationship. Much as I understand where you're coming from and why you didn't disclose your condition until now, it is a serious consideration. Please give me some time to do my own research and consult with my parents. And, Karla, would you mind if I spoke to your doctor?"

We talked a bit more about her condition and how it affected her, and how she felt when she found out. I decided to call my father again. He always knew exactly how to put things into perspective.

"Look, I know this was hard for you to open up about, and I appreciate you telling me. This does not change the way I feel about you. But I do need a few days right now. I'll call you, okay?"

I watched the sunlight fade from her eyes, and my heart contracted.

My emotions were in a whirlwind. Did I want a sick wife? How would this impact her overall functioning? What if she relapsed? Would I become a nursemaid? I was frightened and uncertain. And deeply saddened at the thought that I might lose someone who had become very special to me.

Three days passed. I researched Crohn's, spoke to Dr. R and to my parents. With my heart in my stomach, I gave her a call three days later. Taking a deep breath, I tried reassuring myself. Does anyone really know what type of future awaits them?

"Karla, how are you?"

"Okay," she replied, and I heard uncertainty quivering in her voice.

"Karla, I made my decision." I heard her sharp intake of breath. "I'd like to continue seeing you."

"Oh, Ronny…" she cried.

"It's going to be okay," I soothed. "We're going to get through this- together. Now, I've already been holding this in for three days, so can I please tell you my tantrum story?" She laughed, and I joined her. "I take that as a yes. Well, at nine years old, some boys in my class enjoyed making fun of me. They called me names and ran away, observing my volcanic eruption from a corner. It took a long time and the help of a wonderful school counselor to teach me that my angry reactions were encouraging the very behavior that upset me so much.

"As a sensitive child, it was hard for me to realize that I was merely a puppet in their hands, and would explode or cry at their whim. When I learned tools that empowered me to choose how to respond to provocation, interestingly enough, the bullying stopped. I promised myself that one day I would help children struggling with similar issues.

"Now, in an amazing turnaround, my peers consider me extremely easy-going.

"So, Karla, when you looked at me so nervously a few nights ago, I remembered these lessons from childhood. My goal is to be the kind of guy who makes people feel safe as they communicate what's on their mind, even if it may be a loaded topic. And, this may be premature to say, but I am very interested in hearing your thoughts and feelings.

"Is there any part of me that wished I knew about your situation from the beginning? Yes.

"Do I understand that you were following what you thought was right and respect that? Yes again.

"Am I angry? Not at all. As a matter of fact, I respect you and value the fact that you trusted me to share something private.

"Are you free Saturday night, Karla? I'd love to see you again."

Bittersweet Chocolate

DENISE SPEAKS / MRS. CHOCOLATE
CONFECTION SPEAKS

Denise Speaks:

It's that time of year again- time to start thinking about massive chocolate orders. With two children studying overseas, including one married couple with a baby and one daughter in university, I'd love to spice up their finals season by ordering them something nice. But I also don't want to spend too much. Hm- money always seems to be at the root of my dilemmas.

Oh, look at that! Talk about providence. A company called Chocolate Confection just emailed me, wondering if I need their services this year. I think I used them once before a few years ago to send a birthday gift for a friend. I'll just shoot off a quick response and see if they can do something for both kids that can work within my budget.

Meanwhile, the pace of life is picking up, and I'm feeling pressured by jobs coming at me from all sides. One child's camp application is due, and they want the health form included or they won't look at her application, which means I have to run the form to the doctor and wait for it to be returned before I can send it out. The day school said re-registration must be completed NOW, and in the meantime, our reunion reservation number is growing by the day. We started off as eight people, and we have now increased to one hundred and fifty. And I volunteered to organize this. Okay, Denise, calm down. You're one person and you can only do one job at a time. You'll get it all done. Deep breath, write a list, and tackle each job. Omigoodness- the deadline for my article on juggling older children and younger children while pursuing your own interests is due is three days from now? HELP!

•••

Phew! I got the article out, and the health form has been delivered to our pediatrician. So we're making some progress. Now why hasn't Chocolate Confection responded? It's been a few days already. I guess they can't work within my budget. Okay, I'll try a different company. I really need to get this settled- there's so much to do and so little time to get everything done. There- Marvelous Munchies said they can definitely send packages to both of my children, and they can do it for the price I requested. The order is taken care of, and that's one more thing I can cross off of my list.

Uh-oh. Chocolate Confection just emailed me. They are happy to send both packages, and can do it for the price I requested. I feel bad, but I have to tell them I took my business elsewhere because I didn't hear from them soon enough. I wish I could order from them, too, but that would really defeat my purpose of trying to keep the cost down. Maybe I should have emailed them first and told them that I needed this taken care of within a certain time frame? I hope they won't be too upset.

Upset wasn't the word. Mrs. Chocolate Confection told me she was surprised that I didn't wait for her reply. Don't I remember, she asked, when she went out of her way a few years ago to keep the price within my budget when I made a birthday order? Gulp- I hate conflict. I certainly wasn't trying to upset her by taking business away from someone who was counting on it, nor did I want to show a lack of appreciation for a previous favor. I just needed to get the job done, and I hadn't heard back from her. Turns out she just made a wedding and fell a little behind in her emails... So I question whether or not I made a mistake. I certainly aggravated another person, so right or not, I will apologize. Perhaps I will be clearer in my communication the next time so that such a scenario will not happen again. And perhaps, dear Self, patience is a virtue...on the other hand, this was business, and I was entitled to a clear response in an efficient manner so that I could make my order. Ah, who knows? Did I goof or not?

Mrs. Chocolate Confection Speaks:

What a beautiful wedding! It's hard to believe that our oldest daughter is married. When people told me that the years would fly, I remember smiling politely and wondering if they understood that every sleepless night felt like an eternity. Somehow they were wiser than I recognized at that stage. Sometimes I wonder why the energy and exuberance of youth cannot join with the wisdom of age and experience. It's almost as if we need to enter a new stage as a wide-eyed beginner. Just like with the wedding preparations, I had no idea how all-encompassing it would be. Somehow, I naively believed that I could keep on top of my workload and make a wedding simultaneously. I failed to consider the emotional exhaustion, the placement for over forty out of town guests, and the seemingly endless errands required, attending to every detail, not to mention trying to keep the bride in a calm state while my own tension was sky high. Anyway, there will be time for musing later. Now it's the busiest time of year for beautiful chocolate creations, and every sale will assist us in paying off the debts from this wedding.

I feel fortunate to have work that expresses my creativity and helps people express affection in their relationships. Between so many varied holidays and finals all converging in the month of December, this is my busiest season. Okay, now to check the e-mails and orders and get to work. Amazing! Look how many e-mails with orders accumulated just over this week. I guess the stage of sleepless nights may be recurring. What a blessing to have customers who can value my talent.

One sizzling coffee, one telephone, and one computer ready to take the orders. And one enthusiastic woman ready to give individualized attention and style to each customer. That is my vision and my mission. No two relationships are the same. Therefore, customizing every order to capture a unique flavor of the connection adds that intangible touch which strengthens the warm feelings between people. What a privilege to do this work, but here I go musing again. It's not like me to become so emotional over my everyday tasks. It must be the aftermath of the wedding. My mascara runneth over. Oh well,

I opened an email from a returning client and responded in the affirmative- yes, we would be able to meet her needs. Within seconds my inbox pinged, and apparently I was too late in responding; she had taken her business elsewhere. I responded by explaining the situation, the wedding, being busy. I mean, couldn't she wait three days? She didn't seem to remember the strings I pulled for her the last time she asked. Is there no loyalty anymore?

Well, it appears that even customers that I accorded special discounts in the past became impatient when I did not respond within a few days of their query. Although I can own my mistakes and strive for better service in the future, I still feel pained. Where is their loyalty to the service and quality that I provided? It hurts deeply, emotionally as well as financially. My husband and I were counting on these funds for wedding expenses. Well, there are still some customers on the list. After hearing ten people echo the same sentiments about regretfully taking their business elsewhere, I am ready for a positive infusion. This next lady on the list surely waited for me. She sounded so kind and considerate. She would not be so quick to go elsewhere after all the extra effort I put into serving her the last time.

"Hello, long time no speak. How are you and how is your family? I am pleased to inform you that I can provide for you in the price range you were seeking and quality will not be compromised.

"You went elsewhere, too. I sound upset. Actually, I am. It's difficult for me to understand that just because we were occupied with a family celebration and I got a bit behind, my customers moved on. I thought there was much more of a relationship. And, I thought that, people understand all the different responsibilities that we juggle.

"Yes, it's true that everyone is busy. Sorry for losing it with you. It is just an accumulation of frustration- maybe predominantly with myself. Okay, no hard feelings and have a nice day."

Well, at least I have ten orders, and more may come from some last minute planners.

This is not the mental state I wanted to have right before the busy season. All of this anger and resentment will just poison my heart. Can it be that there is more validity to the other side than I realized?

As a business owner, should I have hired a girl to supervise the emails and respond so that customers felt reassured that their orders were being processed? Perhaps I am being unrealistic. Many businesses that are open one year close the next year, and then they would be in a difficult place with insufficient time to send their orders. No one wants to send a special gift for the holidays after they are finished. Instead of feeling touched, people might feel like an afterthought. Clearly there are many people who appreciate my work. That is a huge blessing. Yes, it would have been nice to have everyone standing in line waiting for me. But am I being just a tad unrealistic in today's frantically paced society and at the busiest time of the year? Particularly the last woman seems like she never wanted to hurt anyone and was almost surprised to hear from me. It appears that she inferred that I could not accommodate her this year.

Yes, holidays are time to strengthen relationships. I can only change myself and need to work on being more attuned to my customers' feelings of urgency. Maybe with the extra time that I now have, I can send each of my customers a special creation just to show there are no hard feelings and that it would be a privilege to serve them in the future.

What a powerful lesson I learned this year. Providing this valuable service for my customers is a serious commitment- one they need to be able to trust. Okay, a fresh cup of coffee, a new coat of mascara, and a positive mindset.

Triangular Trauma

PEGGY SPEAKS / FERN SPEAKS

Peggy Speaks:

"So every time I see a policeman, I freeze, and those traumatic memories get dredged up in my mind. I was arrested, torn from my family, and thrown behind bars for a full thirty hours, and I hadn't done anything wrong! The whole thing was such an insidious mess. So I've been permanently traumatized, and I shake every time I see a police car, not to mention an officer in the flesh. I'm so tired of reliving the situation on such a regular basis. It's over, so why I can't I just move past it? Can you help me?"

My client looked at me pleadingly, and my heart melted for her pain. Hmmm...I tapped my fingers on my desk, deep in thought. She had already come to my office several times, and we had made real headway with her situation; however she was still highly distressed. Perhaps suggesting an adjunct tool could help enhance the pace of her progress and sense of healing. "You know," I told her thoughtfully, "I have a friend who specializes in hypnosis. Does that sound like something you'd be willing to try?"

"I'll do anything," Lisa assured me, and I saw the pain flicker in her eyes.

"Let me call her quickly and see if she can fit you into her schedule."

Lisa waited patiently while I contacted Fern. "No problem," Fern assured me. "Ask her if tomorrow at eleven will work for her?"

"So you're all set," I told Lisa, smiling as I walked her to the door. "Let me know how it works for you, and I'll see you next week."

Admittedly, I harbored a secret fear that I tried to squelch. What if Lisa likes Fern better than me? What if they connect on a deeper level and I become obsolete as Lisa's therapist? And it will be all my doing! Imagine the owner of Kroger directing a customer to Publix for a better shopping experience! The proprietor of Ladies' Workout Express sending a potential client to L.A. Fitness because they have more up-to-date equipment…Why, surely they would have to be seized by temporary insanity to jeopardize their own business! So why did I just send Lisa to another practitioner, pray tell?

The answer is resoundingly clear, and I recognize its clarion call of truth. Ultimately I have my patients' best interests in mind, and I want to help this particular woman conquer her fear and put it behind her. As of yet, she requires more healing. Hypnosis may be the tool that can help her internalize messages of safety and wellbeing on a very deep level beyond what we touch with conventional talk therapy. A wave of calm washed over me as I reassured myself that I had acted properly, truly in the best interest of my client.

"Oh, hi, Lisa, how did it go? Are you calling to schedule our next session? Let me look at my calendar, please- what did you say? We won't be continuing anymore? Why- has something happened? Oh, you really connected to Dr. Fern and feel it would be more beneficial for you to continue your sessions with her? I understand, of course. The main thing is that you've found the proper conduit to help you achieve your goal- I'm very happy for you, Lisa. Yes, I wish you the very best."

I hung up the phone and stared sightlessly ahead. I know I did the right thing, but somehow that knowledge was providing scant comfort to the wound in my soul. Isn't Fern supposed to be my friend? Why didn't she redirect Lisa back to my office? Doesn't she care about me? I would never take away her clients...Oh, come on, Peggy. This is not Fern's fault; it's simply what is best for Lisa. Sigh. Nope- not there yet. Maybe I'll call Fern and see if she can squeeze me in for some hypnosis...

Fern Speaks:

"Sure, Peggy, thanks for thinking of me. It would be a pleasure to team up and work together to help a client. For you, only my best effort will suffice." I decided to research trauma and locate some really effective scripts to help create inner peace and relaxation. It's exciting to share a client with my special friend.

Within just a few sessions Lisa had major breakthroughs.

"Lisa, I am amazed by your progress. It appears that you are no longer haunted by your fear of police. It has been a delight working with you and I wish you continued success. Would you be comfortable sharing what you found most helpful?"

She looked at me, trying to formulate her thoughts, "Well, so many aspects contributed to the picture- let me gather my thoughts. Firstly, I felt comfortable with you immediately as well as a sense of confidence that you would be able to help me. Secondly, the deep breathing and ability to relax is something so new for me. I seem to be a perpetual engine rarely pausing and allowing myself the chance to relax and just live in the moment. In that place of the present moment, breathing in your suggestions of safety and security, I was able to let go of my fear. How can I thank you?"

"You just did! I am so gratified that you responded so well to the hypnosis. Please send Peggy my warmest regards when you see her the next time."

"Actually, I am planning to call Peggy. She is a lovely person and I definitely gained from my work with her. But finding the right therapist who can really help me progress is one essential aspect of the therapy- in some ways, perhaps the most important. And I will be forever grateful to her for leading me to you. But, I cannot afford to see two therapists. So I would like to continue working on issues relating to personal growth with you."

"I am honored by your willingness to trust me and work with me. Please understand that Peggy and I are friends with tremendous regard for one another on a professional level as well. There is an understood protocol that we do not take each other's clients. "

"I understand Peggy is a very spiritual person. I am convinced that she will be happy if I can get more help from you. In fact, I will call her today and let her know of my decision. Even if you refuse to see me, I will not be returning to see Peggy. Once I experienced a method that offers such quick results and helped me so deeply, I cannot return to the other methods with the same motivation. It would not be fair to Peggy or me."

I felt uncomfortable with how the conversation was progressing. "Let's speak tomorrow and give me some time to process your sentiments. Again, congratulations on your hard work. Ultimately, the therapist is only a facilitator. It was your willingness that affected your healing of the trauma. Be well and all the best."

This was an unexpected development. I gave Lisa the benefit of every tool in my arsenal out of love for my friend and colleague, and now I caused Peggy to lose a client. Peggy will feel hurt and betrayed even if I do not continue seeing Lisa. There must be a lesson somewhere. What do I do to repair this potential breach in our relationship? I need to reach out to Peggy and reassure her that this was never my intention. She is a real friend. I hope our relationship can withstand this challenge. I wonder if our roles were reversed, would I find it in my heart to give her my blessings? Would I be able to trust her again?

This is truly agonizing. One part of my heart is filled with joy that I helped a client heal from a trauma that has been destroying her peace of mind. The other part is aching for the pain that I unwittingly caused to my friend. Maybe, I will call Peggy for some of her emotionally focused interventions.

Those are the Brakes

MARK SPEAKS / SCOTT SPEAKS

Mark Speaks:

It was right before winter break when Scott Landow asked me the favor. He's been my best friend since the third grade. His family wanted to go on a vacation outing, but didn't have much money to play with. So Scott had an idea.

"Mark, you know my father's been out of work for a long time, right?"

"Right."

"So, I was wondering- you're going out of town anyway. And my family was talking about going to Silver Lake Trail, but renting bikes is kind of pricey. So I thought, well, maybe I could borrow your bike until you get back."

"Sure," I agreed. "No problem. Enjoy."

I hope he's careful with it. But how could I say no? I've asked him to lend me so many things, and he always says yes...

The Landows were thrilled- all the kids had been able to borrow bikes- and Scott couldn't thank me enough. But when I came back and got on my bike, something was wrong. The brakes weren't working well, and a strange noise sounded each time I tried to pick up speed.

"Did anything happen while you had the bike?" I asked Scott.

"No, it rode fine," Scott assured me. "Thanks for letting me use it. There was a funny kind of noise when I rode really fast, but other than that, it was perfect."

Why in the world, I wondered, *did you keep riding if you heard a strange noise? You should have called me or gotten it checked out. No wonder it's broken!*

Somewhat disconcerted, I took it to the bike shop. I had been generous and tried to do him a favor, but it backfired.

"Three hundred dollars," the technician said, "and we'll have it just like new. But next time," he warned, wagging his finger, "if you hear something unusual, bring it in right away. It's possible that we could have simply tightened the brakes instead of having to replace them, not to mention the tire rim and some other fine tuning."

Gee, thanks. I called Scott and told him what happened.

"I'm so sorry," Scott said. But he didn't offer compensation.

What good does sorry do if you're not going to help pay for damage that you caused?

I didn't know what to do. I did know that I was absolutely furious. He ruined my bike! But he can't afford the repair. After all, Mr. Landow lost his job a year ago. On the other hand, who says I can afford the repair? I don't have three hundred dollars just lying around. Plus I shouldn't have to pay for this! My bike is not a luxury for me- I go everywhere on it. Thoroughly confused, I finally decided to ask my sensei for advice. Why Scott wasn't consumed by guilt was beyond me.

My sensei's words were priceless.

"Of course you're right. Scott was negligent and owes you the money to cover the repair. However, I want you to tell him that he doesn't owe you anything, and that you understand mistakes can happen."

Reaching into the drawer of his large, mahogany desk, my friend pulled out an envelope. With a flourish, he handed me three hundred dollars.

"This is my secret stash that I keep for unexpected, charitable expenses that sometimes crop up," he confided. "I feel this is a worthy cause. Please keep this between us, okay?" Putting a finger on his lips, he gave me a conspiratorial wink.

I have a new respect for my sensei now- what a great guy! But that Scott- I'm still annoyed by his lack of owning up. From what the bike technician said, he should have realized something was wrong before it got so bad. So am I still best friends with him? I don't know- I'll have to think about it. I need a best friend I can trust.

Scott Speaks:

"Mom, can't we do anything exciting during winter break? You should hear what the guys do, and it becomes the talk around school for days. Real exciting stuff! I'm tired of being told there's no money in this family for any fun." I let out a sigh, hoping that my complaining would pay off, but I knew perfectly well that trips were not a priority right now.

"Scott, I am sure this situation is tough on you and everyone in the family. Believe me, Dad and I would love to give our children everything that is good for them. Actually, we did plan an outing this vacation that you will love. There is a beautiful new bike trail and we thought we could all go riding together and then have a picnic."

"I do enjoy biking, Mom, but you're forgetting something. All of us have outgrown our bikes by miles."

"I thought you could each borrow for one day. Chances are the other families will not be using them at the same time. You guys are very responsible and will take good care of them. Isn't your friend Mark going away for the break? You have loaned him our stuff more times than I can count. I'm sure he'd be happy to return the favor."

I perked up right away. Mark would definitely lend me his bike, and he has always been such a great friend. "Okay, Mom, that does sound like a nice plan, and Mom, sorry for complaining. I know you do your best for us. Just sometimes, it's tough being the only one of the guys feeling left out of what sounds like a really good time."

"I hear you, Scott. I accept your apology. You can feel proud of how maturely you have been handling this challenge in general, and hopefully our situation will improve sooner than later."

"Mom, I'm going to head over to Mark's right now to check out this bike idea."

I ran there as quickly as I could, and as I had suspected, he was more than happy to help.

"Scott, I'd be happy to loan you my new 12 speed bike. If there is any guy that's trustworthy, it's you. I can't even count the amount of times, you loaned me your stuff and bailed me out when I didn't have what I needed. Enjoy the bike, courtesy of Uncle Stan. It was thanks to his big check that I got that bike. And have a great winter break. The bike is in great shape- enjoy it."

"Thanks, Mark. It's awesome."

I didn't know if I would ever admit this to the guys, but bike riding was great. I loved racing down the paths and feeling so free. The truth was that I was not really wild over roller coasters, but I wouldn't say it publicly. What kind of wimp got a queasy stomach on a roller coaster- or worse- dared to be scared?

What's that noise coming from the bike? That doesn't sound normal. Mark always told me I worry too much. Didn't he just say it was in great shape? It's probably nothing. It sure doesn't sound like nothing, though.

I wonder if I should mention this noise to Dad. If I do, he'll probably feel a need to pay for repairs and it will be my fault. I know the financial struggle we were having. If I don't mention it and pretend it's a normal noise, aren't I cheating my best friend? Why is everything in life so complicated?

It's possible that Mark didn't realize that something wasn't working properly before he loaned it to me. Who said it was my fault? I sure didn't mistreat it. Maybe Mark, scatterbrain that he is, won't even notice it till the next time he needs a tune up, and then it won't cost any extra money. I thought, Scott, my boy, you got a winner. Bottom line was as much as I prided myself at being a nice guy, I don't want to burden my parents any more. They're suffering enough. I can picture Mom's face when I exploded a few days ago. Every time I close my eyes, I see her pain.

This time, as much as I want to be a good friend, I am choosing to be a good son.

"What noise from the bike? This bike is a beauty, in great working order, just like Mark said. He certainly is the expert of his own bike. Come on, guys, race you to the field where we can have a great game of baseball."

After winter break I got the call that I had been dreading.

"Oh, hi, Mark. Did I notice anything funny when I rode your bike? No, not really? Three hundred dollars? Oh, wow! Nope- it was a Cadillac while I drove it, but I'm sorry that happened to you. Thanks so much for lending it to me- it was amazing."

I started worrying, my thoughts going in circles. *I probably should ask my parents to pay for the damages. But we don't have the money! Mark has two working parents- they can probably afford it. Why should I stress my parents out by telling them we owe three hundred dollars? No- it's definitely better to keep quiet and put this whole thing behind us. I just hope it wasn't my fault...*

On Call

NERVOUS MOM SPEAKS / SAMANTHA SPEAKS

Nervous Mom Speaks:

As an experienced mother of a large family, I don't usually panic or run to the doctor when my children get sick. Most often the virus will run its course, and TLC is usually the best prescription I can offer. However, the other night, when my daughter's feet swelled to twice their normal size in addition to sporting raised red splotches all over her normally creamy skin, I will admit it- I panicked. Do these things ever happen at convenient times? It was 10:30 p.m., and I debated whom to call: the general doctor who is kind, warm, and lives around the corner, or the pediatrician who's a little more formal. I voted for option one.

"Sounds like an allergic reaction," the friendly general doctor said. "Tylenol, Benadryl, and she should be fine. But just in case I'm wrong- I don't deal with childhood ailments- give your pediatrician a call. If he says anything different, will you call me and let me know?"

Thanking him warmly for his advice and feeling mildly relieved, I picked up the phone and dialed Samantha, our pediatrician's wife, who happens to be a friend of mine. We go to the same gym and our kids play together on a regular basis. My heart continued to hammer nervously, especially when I stole another peek at Sylvia's feet, and I looked forward to hearing Sammi's soothing voice.

"Hi, Sammi, how are you?" I began.

"Hi," she replied.

"Is your husband available, by any chance?" I squeaked, fighting to squelch my panic that was rising again.

"Is this a medical question?" Her tone suddenly sounded aloof and business-like.

"Yes," I said, waiting for to pass the phone to her husband.

"He prefers to be called on his pager," she said coldly.

"Aha," I said. "I understand." I got it- really, I did. Boundaries are good, especially when there are people around who can and will easily take advantage. But considering that I'm not one of these types and I can't remember ever calling Dr. Rofatsky at home, I assumed she would let me bow my head under the rope of officialdom and pass on my call to the good doctor.

"Can you give me that number, please?"

"People are supposed to call the office," she replied, and my blood began to boil. Are we friends or not? Have I ever called you like this? Can't you realize that I'm really nervous and just give me the number?

"If you can give me the number now, I will remember to call the office in the future if I need to," I replied, stunned by her attitude.

With a loud sigh she acquiesced, and I paged her husband. When he called and I described my daughter's condition, he curtly asked, "Have you tried Benadryl?" This was in stark contrast to the GP, whose warmth and caring had radiated from his voice, reassuring me that my question was valid and that he was there to help, professionally and as a friend.

Thanking him, I ended our call, and stoked the embers of my fury. How dare she! And I thought we were friends! How many countless times have people called me with their questions, asking me to "do them a favor" and check with my husband. Occasionally I, too, direct them to his office- if it's not urgent, he, too, doesn't always appreciate handling calls at home. But I do my utmost to respond with kindness and concern, never a curt, cold attitude. I know, I know, I can't apply the way I do kindness to someone else. Surely Mrs. Rofatsky does plenty of her own good deeds and this is simply an area where she and her husband jointly decided that a firm hand is required. They probably got burned one time too many before initiating this policy. But I still maintain that one must know with whom she is dealing. Considering the fact that I have never done this before and therefore must really be consumed by worry to breach the normal protocol, I would have at least appreciated a pleasant response.

When I next saw Samantha, I found myself unable to let go and treat her with my normal easygoing manner. I suppose I need some time. Maybe I even woke her up- who knows? Grrr...

Samantha Speaks:

"This just cannot continue. Of course, your devotion is admirable. The whole community values you and needs you. Yet lately the kids and I do not have a husband or father. We have Dr. R. on call, always attached to your pager. We miss you and need to know that we have a priority space with you. When was the last time we had a meaningful conversation that was not interrupted by a mother nervous about her child's condition?"

"Sammi, I hear you and know that kindness begins at home. I have not studied or played with our boys for the longest time.

I thought you dreamed of providing an oasis for anyone in need- to have that open door, just ready to help? I would love to have time off from being Dr. R. and just be your husband and the father of our children."

"This will be difficult to achieve because we have created expectations in our community. No one thinks twice before calling us at any time of day or night. How will we be able to change this? You need time off. You look tired, and for the first time I notice you nodding in agreement that something needs to change."

"It's true and changing those practices is going to require a special plan that we stick to with total commitment. Samantha, I'm ready when you are, but trust me, this will be very difficult for both of us. It will require setting strict boundaries and enforcing them consistently without exception in the beginning. Once the expectation is no longer there, we will be free to make occasional exceptions for really desperate situations. However, let's think about this logically. A parent with a sick child after hours has the option to go to an urgent care center, a hospital, or call the pager for whichever doctor is on call at that time. A doctor has the right to have a life after work and his family has the right to his time and attention."

This conversation gives me hope, yet both of us are such softies. Perhaps, we have to expect obstacles and create a plan to help us overcome them.

Okay, let's brainstorm some potential obstacles.

*Nervous first-time mothers who are literally panicking

*Parents who assure you it is only a quick question

*Parents who have a friendly relationship with us so they feel free to expect the extra mile

*Children themselves who feel comfortable enough coming with questions

*Grandparents who do not want to interfere with the questionable child raising practices of their children, but…

*Parents of adult children nervous about any risk factors their children may encounter as they leave the safety of their nest

*Young adults

*Parents who do not use our practice, yet want advice and second opinions

*Teachers and principals who want ideas for their science fair projects

*Spouses having conflicts about the health decisions for their families and want us to mediate or choose the "winner" of the argument with our superior medical judgment

*Families that want us to justify the unhealthy eating and sleeping habits of their family with data

*Lonely people who just want to talk

Wow. This is eye opening. If these are the obstacles we envision after only a couple of minutes of thinking, certainly there must be many others lurking. Clearly, if we have a different policy for each obstacle, people will feel hurt and confused. Our community is small and some will say that they can call us at home and there is no problem, while others will feel rejected.

"Sammi, this will be hard for you, as you are warmth personified. But we both know there is only one way to recalibrate our family life, which is so important to all of us. At least initially, we must have a clear, no exceptions policy of separation between home and work. No matter who calls, they must be asked politely to call my pager and then I can take care of it accordingly. As we change the system, we need to be prepared that any change is always challenging, yet our motives are pure- the protection of our family life, which has gotten severely diminished with our current system. It may require us to experience discomfort and perhaps even anger from some of our patients and neighbors who we have trained to expect differently from us. Are we ready for this?"

"Yes, we are. I know it will be tough, yet our family needs this. This plan is a life preserver in turbulent waters."

He smiled at me, "It already helps to know that we share the same values and that this evolved because we both want to do good."

I felt a buzzing in my pocket, "Interestingly enough, my cell is ringing. Oh, it's only my friend, though it may be my very first challenge.

"Hi, how are you? You want to speak to my husband?" My mood soured quickly.

I thought to myself, "Why did my first challenge have to be a friend who does not ordinarily call? We made a deal and consistency in all situations is an integral part of its success. I must be firm and clear. I did not realize how painfully difficult this would be. It's almost as if I need to turn off my natural switch for compassion. Maybe, no, I must keep affirming-compassion to family first. Okay, remember the greater good, plus people have a host of other options. And remember the first time will be the hardest. I have to just be a tape recorder playing a businesswoman. I can do this."

I took a breath to steel my nerves. "Yes, I am sorry, but my husband prefers to receive all medical calls to his business. Thank you for your understanding and have a pleasant evening."

The Extra Mile

TARA SPEAKS / BECKY SPEAKS

Tara Speaks:

Becky and I had been friends forever. We walked each other through the minor and major tribulations of raising our families, always there for each other. But during the last few years, our relationship became more one-sided. After years of roller-coastering in a tumultuous marriage, Becky and Bruce finally divorced. She needed a lot of support to get through that trying time, especially when Bruce remarried shortly after the divorce was finalized.

Time passed, and Becky moved on, literally and figuratively. Packing up her house of almost twenty years, she decided to move to Brooklyn and create a new life for herself. She and Bruce had lived there a number of years ago, so she already had friends there and liked the area. Watching her go tore a piece from my heart, but I knew it was the best thing for her and her family to create a fresh beginning. In an awesome display of providence, her new husband awaited her there, and a year after her move, she called me to share the amazing news that she was engaged.

"It would mean the world to me if you came to my wedding," she told me. How could I not go? I'm not a big traveler and flights are expensive, but what don't you do for a lifetime friend?

Two weeks before the wedding I left her a message that I had a ticket.

"I can't wait to see you!" she texted me.

A text? Can't she even pick up the phone and tell me that I made her day?

Assuming she would arrange for my transportation to and from the airport as I have always done for my out of town guests who joined us for special occasions, I waited to hear who would be picking me up. When no message was forthcoming, I finally called her.

"Becky, do you have someone who can get me from the airport?" I asked.

"I really don't know anyone I can ask," she replied, casually shrugging off the responsibility.

My temper started to flare, and I struggled to keep my voice neutral. Why couldn't she ask her fiancé if he knew anyone? Or at least offer to handle the expense if I had to get a taxi? After all, she was marrying someone who had a lucrative job.

"Becky, I can't really afford to pay a taxi on top of my airline ticket," I pressed. "So I'm not sure what to do now."

Finally she got the hint and arranged for a car service to pick me up, splitting the cost with me. I felt she should have covered the whole tab, but I let it go and thanked her graciously.

The wedding was poignant and beautiful, and I was so glad that I was able to be there with her. Watching her summon the strength to leave her tattered past behind and step into a hopeful future, I could only wipe my streaming eyes and pray as I gazed at her standing beside her new husband on the podium.

The next day, the same car service spirited me back to the airport, and in short order I found myself back home and thankfully re-immersed in my routine. Every so often I would think about Becky and wonder how she was managing, but we didn't talk much over the next few months. Assuming she was busy building her new home, I didn't take it too personally when my calls weren't returned. And then the call came.

"Tara, I'm coming in for Robin's wedding," Becky informed me.

"Great!" I said, excited that we'd have a chance to reconnect.

Robin was our mutual close friend, and her first child was getting married.

"I was wondering," she continued, "do you think you could give Bruce and me a ride to the airport on Sunday?"

Now, now, Tara, simmer down. You know revenge is a no-no. Simply because she had to be practically coerced to help you with your airport transportation when you were coming in for her wedding is not an excuse to say no to her request. You know that, right?

"Let me check my schedule and get back to you," I told her, needing some time to formulate my response.

Since I didn't want to suffer guilt pangs for taking revenge, although I admit I was somewhat tempted, I knew I would say yes. However, since my children were off on Sunday, I didn't want to be saddled with a carpool in the middle of the day and disrupt our whole schedule.

"I can take you earlier than you need to go," I offered, "but I have to be home by 1:30."

Becky hemmed, double-checking that I couldn't take them any later, and wound up getting another friend to give them a ride so they wouldn't have to hang out for hours at the airport.

I breathed a sigh of relief, feeling I had done my part yet maintained a healthy boundary.

I imagined what I would say to her if I had the courage. *Becky, I'll always love you and wish only good things for you. But once upon a time we were there for each other. And I miss that.*

Becky Speaks:

Who would have believed after all the turmoil that I would get another chance at happiness with such a wonderful guy? I must share this news with Tara. She really stood by my side through each and every excruciating part of my journey.

Amazing! It sounds like Tara will come to the wedding. I am so totally overwhelmed making a wedding in a new city. It is so different this time around, when I am not just the prop and parents deal with all the technical details. Now, I am the bride and the wedding planner. I wish I had a friend like Tara locally who could hold my hand through all the details and squeeze when needed.

Emotionally everything is also so different this time around. The first time I entered naively with the assumption that people who get married stay married and live happily ever after. Now after having gone through turbulence, I feel scared. I am also worried about the children. Will this new marriage affect them negatively? I always want them to feel welcome in my home. Some children feel they have no home when their parents remarry and wonder about where they fit into the equation. Isn't it amazing that more homes can mean less sometimes?

How can I cope with all of these racing thoughts and calls to the makeup lady, hair lady, caterer, band, and of course make time for my fiancé and allow him to think that I have my act together?

Now, let me go through the response cards, phone messages, and texts. With today's technology, people respond in a variety of ways and the caterer is pressuring me for an exact head count. Some people write some heartfelt messages. I wish I had the presence of mind to respond in kind, but I am sure they understand.

Oh, look, here's a phone message from my dear friend, Tara, and she is coming. I wish I could have a nice chat with her instead of all the other "to do's" on the list. Yet I know what happens when I call her... a few minutes so easily turns into an hour, which I just can't spare right at the moment. At least I will text her and let her know how excited I am to have her there at my wedding. "Dear Tara, can't wait to see you!" If anyone understands busy, it's dear Tara. And she is certainly not one to bear a grudge.

Let's see- is it possible that I am forgetting any details? Luckily this is not a Cleveland wedding. When I lived in Cleveland, the protocol was to organize transportation for all of the out of town guests, but here there are so many weddings- that would just be impossible. I don't know people in this community yet, and it is too soon to ask my fiancé to impose on his family when that is not done in this community. Tara has not said a word yet- she probably understands and has no such expectations. Oh, look who's calling- it's Tara! 'Hi, how are you? So excited you will be sharing the big day with me. I miss you.

"You are wondering about transportation. Oh, funny you should ask. It's not done here in this community, so if you want, I will split the car service if it's difficult for you, although wedding expenses are mounting. I wish I could pick you up, but I guess on my wedding day there are some other commitments I must attend to. Thanks for understanding, Tara. You're the greatest!"

●●●

Congratulations! I am married to a wonderful guy. A second chance for happiness. Thank you, G-d, for bringing me to this point.

"Bruce, I am looking forward to showing you around Cleveland. You would not believe the suburban mentality. They wait on you hand and foot. I actually kind of miss that lifestyle. I can just call friends and ask them to do an airport run and it's a non-issue. A person like Tara has always been there for me would drop everything to do this kindness. I will call her right now." I pulled out my phone, excited to talk to my friend. I have been so busy setting up my home, and making my children comfortable that I have no time for a social life.

"Hi, Tara, long time, no speak! What does your schedule look like on Sunday? How would you like the privilege of bringing me and my wonderful new husband to the airport?"

Ruling My Roost

JILL SPEAKS / JASMINE SPEAKS

Jill Speaks:

"Good night, sweetie," I said, bending down to plant a kiss on little Alan's cheek. "Sleep well."

Closing his door halfway, I breathed a sigh of relief. Phew! Alan and Stephanie are down, baby's quiet, so now I can hand the kids over to Rob and run to my weekly parenting class. The psychologist, Dr. Spotts, always has so much to give over; I wondered what her topic would be this time.

The class seemed to fly by in minutes, even though it was over an hour long. Wow- what a class! It was really up my alley, too. Dr. Spotts stressed the importance of structure and orderliness in children's lives, reiterating how they should have a schedule for mealtimes, school work, bedtime, and really for just about everything that happens during their day. She says this will help them become organized adults who can function effectively in the real world. Equally important, she said, is for them to take care of their belongings and have a set place where they keep each of their things.

"Have you ever seen," the doctor asked, a small smile playing on her lips, "the mother who's trying to herd her brood out the door, and little Molly suddenly appears wearing her jacket but no shoes? The mother's face turns red, and she gets flustered, repeatedly glancing at her watch as her tension grows. 'We're going to be late,' she announces, her words sounding like staccato notes. Her tension increases as the frantic search for shoes ensues..."

Chuckles filled the room as the group nodded knowingly. It seemed like a familiar picture to many. But I straightened my shoulders and determined that this would never resemble the portrait of my home. I will rule my roost- my roost will not rule me.

Armed with determination to transform my basically organized home into tip-top shape, I began writing lists as soon as I got home. My children will learn to value the importance of time and organization.

"Okay, kids," I told Stephanie and Alan the next afternoon, "line up all of your riding toys under the stairwell. Then you can come up and eat lunch."

"But Mom," Stephanie protested. "It takes so much longer to get them out if we put them over there. Can't we just leave them out?"

"Absolutely not," I retorted, working hard to keep my voice calm while my insides churned. Will Stephanie be my black sheep? I hope she won't be the one who can't find her missing shoe just when it's time to go, making the whole family late for school. Or her homework, or her lunch...what a disaster! I shuddered and squared my shoulders. Not if I can help it, I determined.

"No lunch until every toy is put in its place," I reiterated firmly, priding myself on staying resolute and maintaining my standards.

"Can you read me a story?" Alan pulled on my skirt a little later, holding his favorite book, *The Royal Mission*.

I checked my watch and then my list.

"No sweetie, I'm sorry," I told him, patting his shoulder. "I have to start making dinner now so it can be ready on time."

Because if dinner is served late, baths will be late, bedtime will run later, and we may all oversleep the next day, and what a disaster that would be! Not to mention the fact that everyone will be moody and irritable all day.

Turning towards the stove to begin making dinner, I caught the sad slump of Alan's shoulders as he shuffled away. He'll be grateful when he's old enough to understand, I assured myself, deftly dicing some vegetables and tossing them into the frying pan.

The week flew by, replete with my solid attempts of keeping order every step of the way. I wondered what Dr. Spotts would speak about this time.

I quickly and efficiently served dinner and was working hard on the bedtime routine so I could attend another fabulous lecture. Suddenly, a knock sounded on my door.

"Hi, Jill." It was my neighbor, Jasmine. "Can I borrow an onion?"

Masking my disapproval, I pasted a smile on my face and went to get her the onion. If she had made a proper shopping list, I was sure she would not have needed to borrow such a staple. And anyway, why is she just starting to cook dinner now?

"Here you go," I said, handing it over as I closed my door.

Yikes! I'm five minutes behind because of the onion interruption. What will the others think if I show up late for the class?

"Alan, out of the bath already! It's Stephanie's turn!" I yelled.

"But I'm playing," he protested, making honking noises as he steered his boat around the bathtub.

Having his best interests in mind, I yanked the toy out of his hand and flipped the lever, letting the water swish down the drain.

"Bath time is over, darling. We have to get you to bed."

Carrying a howling towel clad Alan, I promptly began putting on his pajamas. If I try really hard, I should still be able to make it on time.

Slightly out of breath, I made it! So there wasn't time for bedtime stories tonight, I mused, sliding into my seat. But I know I'll come back recharged after culling some new wisdom on how to run my home in the best possible way. What better gift can I give my family?

Fabulous, just amazing, I thought, coming home and opening the door to my complex. As I walked in, I tripped, finding my balance just before I fell into an unceremonious heap. That was close, I thought, clutching the banister and breathing hard. But what was that? I stared in horror as I realized exactly what **IT** was. Why, Jasmine's kids had left all of their riding toys all over the place! Where exactly did that leave a path for us to walk? Didn't she ever hear the words order and organization? Apparently not! I will call her immediately and tell her that it's simply not acceptable to have such a lackadaisical attitude. Even if she's not worried about her children's future, she still has to prioritize the safety of the other residents in our building!

Marching up the stairs and planning exactly what I would tell her, I passed by her apartment and heard children's voices.

What in the world are they doing up at this hour? I wondered, horrified. This situation was going from bad to worse. After I tell her my piece, maybe I'll invite her to join me for Dr. Spotts' next lecture. She can really use the help...

Jasmine Speaks:

My garbage can overflows with crumpled up notes with words unspoken to my neighbor, Jill. The emotional intensity reminiscent of high school allowed the escape of a small smile, quickly masked by the angst of feeling judged and misunderstood. Ever friendly and optimistic Jasmine, they called me, the girl who never needed an umbrella because it just would not rain, although I did get drenched at times. The girl who was elected peacemaker because of a severe allergy to conflict of any kind is dreaming of relocating to her own house away from the hustle bustle of apartment life. What is happening in my internal world?

I am a young girl again and dreading Sundays because my sister and I had to clean the whole house before we were allowed to make any social arrangements. My sister seemed to actually enjoy the chores, while the mop and vacuum taunted me and kept me away from playing with my friends. I promised myself that my children would not grow up with that experience, and so they don't.

Yet, somehow I wound up in an apartment building with a very sweet neighbor who wants to control our public living area. I am happy to let my darling children leave their bikes parked on a slant and enjoy the carefree time of being children. Of course, I enjoy the rare occasion when my house is neat. Yet, there are priorities. I choose nurturing my children over rigid structure that does not allow them the wings to fly. They revel in my love and there is no tension in their cute, little pudgy shoulders as they race around on their riding toys, singing at top volume. Our bedtime hour is from seven to eleven, and each child gets a private conversation about his day and his feelings. And we do not have pantry locks so that my children can experience a full kinesthetic experience with each texture. And when they experiment cleaning up the confectionary sugar on the kitchen floor with water, well the icing can rival the best recipes in any cookbook and the camera captures their antics for posterity. My apartment would not win an award in a good housekeeping periodical, but the sounds of laughter echoing out of it bring a smile to many faces.

Jill seems to believe that she must teach me how to educate my children. When I came home from the park yesterday with a long list of phone calls to make, she greeted me with a smile and a mop- yes, that old instrument of torture. She suggested that we clean the common areas together and stack up the toys in a perfect line by 5:00 every day so that dinner can follow, and then baths and bed time- like clockwork.

If she wants to raise toy soldiers all in a row, that is her prerogative. I see the yearning in her children's eyes when they see my children playing gleefully in the sand, unrestrained by warnings of stains or time alerts every five minutes.

The last thing I want is confrontation with Jill, yet her insistence on one approach is triggering intense emotion, and yes, on a deeper level, feelings of inadequacy. I never could keep things tidy like my sister. Somehow, mess challenged me and there were always so many more enjoyable activities that beckoned, tempting me to procrastinate that which I found so distasteful and utterly unstimulating. And besides, how can Jill be so sure that when raising young children, total adherence to tidiness does not cramp their style?

Maybe I should call the parenting expert, Dr. Spotts, and give her a bit of information so that Jill and her children can receive the guidance that they need. Why should I have to run away when I am not imposing my style on anyone? Now that's a good idea.

Ever optimistic Jasmine is making a comeback.

"Hello, Dr. Spotts, it's Jasmine Marks calling. I need your help with a situation in my apartment building."

Book-Nook

ANNA SPEAKS / MRS. MEKOVSKY SPEAKS:

Anna Speaks:

Nestled in a small corner plaza centrally located in the small, urban community of Rolling Hills, Book-Nook was the place to pick up the newest books and other assorted household items. Owned and managed by the Mekovskys, the little store had been a fixture in town for almost as long as Anna could remember. When the Mekovskys first showed up in the neighborhood, Anna felt charmed by their sweet mannerisms and wanted to help this immigrant family succeed. Her heart ached for all of the difficulties they would encounter as Russians trying to merge into the big American melting pot, and she felt driven to ease their plight. Hadn't they suffered enough in Russia, she remembered thinking. And who could know what one person could do for another when she set her mind to it?

When she invited them for dinner a lifetime ago, they told her they were both doctors in Russia, but couldn't practice in the U.S. without going back to school.

"But we have to pay the bills," they spoke in thick accents. "We don't have money."

For the next few weeks the Mekovskys embedded themselves in Anna's mind. She felt driven to help them, but couldn't figure out what to do to ease their transition. Until she stopped by their home one Friday to deliver a cake and got the answer she was looking for.

A collection of old books and beautiful silver, antique ornaments lined one wall of their modest living room. And suddenly, Anna had a brainstorm.

"You know what Rolling Hills needs?" Anna exclaimed. "A combination book and gift store would fill such a void here! It's the perfect thing, and I think you'll be amazingly successful! I know you will! And people will love picking up these novelty items that you've collected, too- I just know the silver items will be a big hit."

On the wings of prayer and with tremendous effort, Book-Nook was born. Mrs. Mekovsky always had a cheerful greeting for all of her clientele. But lately, Anna noticed a worried frown sitting on Mrs. Mekovsky's lips, and when she popped into Book-Nook from time to time, it was impossible to ignore the glaring void of customers. Opening the bookstore's glass door one afternoon, a loud silence enveloped her, and her heart constricted.

"How are you, Mrs. Mekovsky?" Anna ventured to the older Russian lady, hoping to see the trademark smile on her lips.

A loud sigh answered her question.

"Business is not so good," Mrs. Mekovsky confided. "I'm wondering if we will have to close our doors."

Anna gasped and put a hand over her mouth.

"But we need you!" she protested. "Rolling Hills wouldn't be the same without you!"

A pile of guilt settled on Anna's shoulders as her well-meaning advice from way back resounded in her mind. *Was this her fault? Had she led this sweet, innocent family down the wrong path?*

"Ach!" Mrs. Mekovsky waved a tired hand, as if brushing away Anna's protests. "These days everyone gets what they need online. It's easier, just a click of a button, and poof! It comes straight to their house. When we first emigrated many years ago, we filled a need. But now, maybe it's time to face the facts- we are not wanted anymore."

Anna swallowed over a hard lump in her throat. This was terrible! With courage and determination, they had built up a small family business, and concurrent with its growth was their stepping up the ladder in becoming integrated Americans. And now, would they be forced to begin anew again? And at this point, in their older years? Where was the loyalty owed to them?

"It's probably just a dry spell," Anna soothed, wanting to wipe the pain from Mrs. Mekovsky's deep brown eyes. "You'll see."

"No," Mrs. Mekovsky rejoined in a hard, disappointed tone. "It's been like this for a long time already. Right before a holiday the store is busy. But in between?" With a sweep of her arm, she gestured to the empty store. "It's like this."

While Anna browsed the shelves in search of a new book, her mind wandered.

Why would people be so disloyal? Don't they see the obligation to support local proprietors? I just don't understand it. Not overly computer savvy, Anna couldn't relate to the pull of internet shopping. *What's so difficult about a five-minute drive?* She shook her head, pronouncing judgment on her community. *It's just not right*, she thought, shaking her head with frustration.

"Have a good day, Mrs. Mekovsky," Anna wished her. "I hope things pick up."

Mrs. Mekovsky flashed a small smile, but it didn't reach her eyes.

Later that afternoon, Anna's daughter, Dina, came home from school bursting with excitement.

"Mom, there's this amazing new game out that I'd really love to get before our class overnight! Everyone's talking about it. But my friends told me you can only order it in online. Can we use your work computer and order it? Please? Please?"

"Are you sure Book-Nook doesn't have it?" Anna asked, seeing Mrs. Mekovsky's woebegone expression in her mind's eye. "They do carry some games and novelty items, too."

"They definitely won't have it! And by the time they would order it and get it in, it would be too late- I'd never have it in time. Please, Mom? Can I show you the website?"

Leading Dina into the study, Anna watched as her daughter deftly pushed buttons and the right website sprang up in seconds.

"See?" Dina bubbled, "It's only fifteen dollars, and there's even free shipping if you order today. Okay, Mom?"

Giving her the green light, Dina ordered the game and left the study humming happily.

That really was quick and easy, Anna mused, sautéing some vegetables to go with supper. *Omigoodness! April's birthday is next week, and I didn't get her a gift yet!* April was turning 19 and attending her second year of college in Baltimore. *Hey! Maybe I can order a book online and get it shipped!*

Anna, she chided herself as she poured spices on the chicken. *What happened to loyalty? Book-Nook, remember? Go over there, pick out a book, run to the post office...*Anna sighed. *But I have so much to do this week. What harm can there be if I just peek and see if I find anything?* And while supper was cooking, Anna opened her browser, found a brand new historical novel that was just

April's type, and in a manner of minutes, the purchase, shipping, and handling were all wrapped up.

Hmm...a pang of guilt pierced her heart. Did I just do something wrong? Now that I see how easy it is, I can understand the inclination to do my shopping this way. Does that make me guilty of disloyalty, also? Will I bear responsibility along with the community if Book-Nook has to close its doors? No, Anna told herself firmly. *This is just a one-time aberration. If they go out of business, it will have nothing to do with me.*

A few days later Anna passed her calendar and noticed that she had an engagement celebration to attend the following Tuesday evening. *Good thing I looked; I totally forgot about it!* Relief quickly changed to discomfort. *I never got a gift. How can I show up without a gift?* There was absolutely no way she would have time to run to Book-Nook during the next few days. She was backlogged at work, even putting in overtime, and from the moment she got home, she would be steamrolled quickly through supper, homework, and bedtime, occasionally finding time to take a few breaths.

What should I do? And then it came to her: NewBooksPlus.org, a great place for your gift needs...They were perfect when I ordered April's gift. Maybe just this once, Anna told herself. *Or twice, but who's counting? After all, this is an extenuating circumstance, and they'll have it shipped to me in two days.*

That Tuesday evening, Anna and her husband entered the hall and placed their gift on the large table brimming with colorfully wrapped presents.

"Hello, Anna."

"Mrs. Mekovsky, how are you?"

"Managing, Anna, thank you. And you?"

Omigoodness, she knows! She saw me put down a gift, and she knows I didn't get it from Book-Nook! Oh, why did I have to run into her now? Should I explain? Not say anything? Beg for her understanding and tell her this was a one-time deviation, reassuring her that I'm staunchly loyal through and through?

As Anna was embroiled in internal debate, she glanced at Mrs. Mekovsky, and what she saw made her flinch. The raw pain in her eyes was unmistakable, and Anna wished she could run for cover. Couldn't her cell phone ring or one of her friends come bounding out to extricate her from this mess?

Mrs. Mekovsky Speaks:

I wonder what is wrong with me lately. It's just one long sigh after another, broken up by the occasional low moan. Life was so much harder in Russia. Everyone lived in constant fear of who might be an enemy. We did not even know if our children would turn against us. The indoctrination of the Soviet educational system brainwashed many people against any other loyalty. Hard work was the lifestyle to earn even the barest minimum, yet one complaint never escaped my lips. Who would dare to utter a complaint in this Soviet paradise?

Rest and relaxation were as much of a second language as English. Terms and concepts like vacation or leisure time could not enter my brain despite advanced educational degrees. I remember the first time being invited as a guest for dinner, and the family members actually laughed together. That was probably a turning point for me. People laughed comfortably and no one was scared or looked furtively behind and quickly pretended it was a coughing fit. I remember the first time our family laughed together- the sound was so different, I nearly called a doctor to make sure those sounds emanating from our throats were not harmful. My husband, who was a very prominent doctor back in Russia, reassured me it was not worrisome or dangerous- but contagious- yes!

Another sigh! America made me a softie. Suddenly, hardship and pain are strangers. America gave us so many opportunities that we did not have in Russia. The taste of freedom is intoxicating. So many flavors, so many choices…

Then I wonder guiltily, maybe Russia had a point. What do people do with all these choices? They are bombarded with advertisements and competition, which only distracts them… and then an old fashioned book store practically loses its charm with proximity to the endless possibilities winking at customers and casting their alluring spell.

I remember when the bookstore idea came up. My husband and I argued vehemently that the idea of Russian immigrants owning and managing a bookstore is incongruous. How can we advise customers? We did not count on Anna's persuasive talents and her confidence. She believed that my husband's innate wisdom coupled with his photographic memory would create a very inspirational brand for our community's bookstore. And, initially she seemed right! Anyway, this musing is so American—let me clear my mind and enjoy the festivities tonight.

Maybe when the community sees me, they will remember their good old-fashioned homegrown book and gift store.

And, I can always enjoy a nice chat with Anna. If there is anyone that I totally trust, who does not get swept along this tidal wave of everything at your fingertips with the touch of a button, it is she. I think I might pluck up the courage to speak to her about my feelings.

Anna's face looks pale and riddled in guilt. "Anna, not you too! The one person I thought had her life vest tightly fastened so as not to get swept away by the lure of instant …

"I was planning on speaking to you and sharing my real concerns and getting your advice," I continued. "You helped us the first time. We might need new career guidance. I guess that you resisted as long as possible."

"Wait, I can explain, it's not what it appears, it was just a one-time fling," Anna protested. "I am loyal and do believe in supporting your efforts and the ideals of having a local book store."

"Anna, you don't understand; it's even harder now than before because we don't have the energy to begin all over again. I came to participate in this occasion, but just one glance at the gift table tells a story- a story of technology- a story of busy people who want all the convenience that only on-line can offer. And, we just simply cannot compete with that- nor am I sure that we want to…"

"Mrs. Mekovsky, please listen," Anna begged.

"Anna, I listened to your assurances before and look where that got us. Forgive me, but I will leave now. Maybe Russia had a point in teaching people not to trust because they will turn their backs on you when you have outgrown your usefulness to them. Anna, I thought you were the exception!"

Now that I am home, I feel terrible about my outburst to Anna. I was shocked, yet she did seem to genuinely care. Her eyes filled with tears when I told her I can't trust her. Can I allow myself to trust her? Maybe the situation is not black or white, soviet or capitalist. Maybe, there can still be hope. Maybe there can be a solution…

A Work Of Art

GAIL SPEAKS / THE BOSS SPEAKS:

Gail Speaks:

Running nervous fingers through her wavy, auburn hair, Gail took a deep breath and hoped that her artwork was at last satisfactory. She had worked long and hard on the cover jacket for Mark Bell's new book, and lost track of the amount of changes they had attempted over the last few weeks. Communication whizzed through the air as she tried, time after time, to pacify Mark's grandiose vision while trying to maintain a presentation of dignity and subtlety. Lifting her almond eyes to look at the computer screen, she breathed a sigh of relief and allowed herself a slight smile. *This one was good, really good.* She had a strong feeling that both her boss and Mark would be satisfied, at last. The idea had flown into her mind late last night, robbing her of much needed sleep, and at four in the morning, she finally tossed her comforter aside and slid into her computer chair. And now, finally, just as the first hues of sunrise streaked the sky, her design was born. It was an amazing thing, really, to see a picture in your mind take physical form and shape and become reality.

Time for a break, Gail decided, noting the time. Seven a.m.- there was time for at least one cup of coffee before six-month-old Sally and four-year-old Joey would awaken and demand their due.

"Hi, Helene, how are you?"

Sitting at the oval kitchen table overlooking her deck, Gail relaxed and decided to check in with her best friend.

"Too early to tell. I'm starting my diet today, and I'm already hungry. On another note, Gail, I wanted to let you know that Sunrise Magazine's graphic designer is leaving. I already put in a good word for you to my boss. Wouldn't that be amazing if we could be co-workers?"

"Interesting," Gail replied haltingly. "I mean it would be fabulous, actually. I would have to see what's involved."

"Well, of course," Helene said. "But don't be surprised if you get an email or a phone call from Dave Fipps about the position. I really hope you get it."

"Thanks, Helene," Gail said. "You're a real friend."

A new job? She had been working for Wings Publications for five years, ever since graduating college. The hours were convenient- she was able to send the children off in the morning and pick them up by three p.m., and the pay, while she would love to see an increase (who wouldn't?) was satisfactory. She knew her way around Wings, had friends and pleasant relationships with co-workers, and enjoyed a respectful relationship with her boss. If she were offered a new job with Sunrise, a much more prestigious company, would she- should she- take it?

Let's not jump ahead, she cautioned herself. *After all, you haven't even gotten an offer yet. For all you know, there's a mile long list of potential graphic artists who have much more impressive qualifications.*

Quickly closing the window on her musings, she downed the last drops of her coffee just as Sally and Joey began to harmonize their wake-up calls.

The email was not long in coming. During a mid-morning break, Gail's heart began beating rapidly as she grazed over the note from Sunrise.

Dear Mrs. Blass,

Sunrise is seeking a talented graphic artist to fill a recently vacated position. Your work comes highly recommended, and I wondered if we could set up a time to meet and discuss possible employment.

Looking forward to hearing from you,

David Fipps

Executive Editor, Sunrise Weekly Magazine

Well, there's certainly no harm in meeting, Gail decided, rapidly sending a note in response.

Several days later, Gail wandered around in a fog. Sunrise had offered her a position that required only two hours more a day than her current job, but the salary was significantly higher. Their system was much more high-tech than what Gail was used to; it would be like learning a whole new language. Was she up to that challenge? Should she trade in her veteran status in her current job, where people respected her abilities, for a job where she would begin as a novice, having to learn everything from scratch?

The possibility was intriguing. On the other hand, her Grandma always used to say, "If it's not broken, why fix it?"

On the other hand (she was grateful that she only had two hands), if the opportunity presented itself, perhaps it was foolish to say no. Certainly as the kids got older, a larger income would be helpful, even necessary. And she was blessed with a wonderful babysitter who was almost part of the family- Bella would be only too happy to stay the extra hours, and the children would be happy and well-cared for. Shaking her head, she tried to dismiss her mother's disapproval of such a situation. After all, her mother had been a stay-at-home Mom, firmly insisting "Children belong with their Mama." As it was, her mother thought she was away for too many hours. Shuddering, she decided to cross that bridge if and when she came to it.

A ping in her inbox distracted her from her quandary.

"Gail, the cover jacket is amazing! Outstanding work- thank-you! Mark"

Smiling, Gail replied to the author's gratitude. And then a note from her boss quickly followed: "Knew you could bring it to life. Tom"

Wow! Talk about timing! Should she give up security, comfort, and reputation? They were managing just fine on her salary now- why rock the boat? But these opportunities don't come up all the time. Perhaps if she didn't grasp it now, a time would come when they would need it and it wouldn't be available. What to do?

Picturing an Olympic size pool, Gail felt like she was poised, about to dive in. That first immersion was always an icy shock, but after that, her body would adjust, and the water would feel deliciously invigorating.

She could ask her husband, but she knew he would toss the ball right back in her court, telling her this was her decision since it would mostly affect her.

And what about loyalty? Wings had hired her fresh out of college, believing in her potential. No other agency would even glance at her at that early stage. Ever so patiently, they guided her to her current level of expertise. Was it fair to now transfer that expertise to a more prestigious company?

Chocolate, she decided. *It always helps me gain clarity, not to mention other things.*

Okay, here goes. I'm writing a list of pros and cons. I knew the chocolate would help me figure things out.

Pros:

*Better salary

*Finance private school tuitions when the time comes

*Save up for a house

*Prestigious Company- good for reputation- nice addition to resume

*Opening door to learning new skills and stepping up in my career

Cons:

*More hours- will I be too tired to have patience for the kids? Will they miss me too much or be Mommy deprived, even though they love Bella? Am I reneging on my most important career for the allure of some jingling coins and prestige?

*Where is my loyalty to Wings who planted me, watered me, and helped me grow?

*Fear- what if I don't succeed in my new position? Am I relinquishing a secure job for an unknown? And, if I fail, will I wind up with nothing?

I have to discuss this with my hubby, Gail mused, in between creamy bites. But there is a convincing whisper pushing me to move onwards and upwards. After all, why were we put in this world if not to move forward? We weren't put here to remain robots, comfortably ensconced in the same place our whole lives, performing only tried and true tasks without reaching up to grasp new opportunities.

I think, she mused, looking with regret at the empty wrapper, *I'm inclined to go for the gold. I might need more chocolate to face my boss after presenting my resignation. And then, oh no, there's Mommy- more chocolate? I wonder what diet Helene's on...But Gail, get a hold of yourself! You were just offered a job with a leading publishing company. You're going places, my friend, and it's wonderfully exciting. I can't wait to tell the hub! Ready or not, Sunrise, here I come!*

The Boss Speaks:

Every now and again, there is a genuine satisfying feeling when you take a risk, give a beginner a chance and see the growth and development. I remember when we needed a graphic designer and there were so many applicants for the position. Many had experience and definite styles and undoubtedly could have done a beautiful job for our fledgling publishing company. Yet something about Gail's innocence and hopeful eyes as she showed her impressive portfolio pulled at my heartstrings. Her youthful enthusiasm, refreshing openness to learning, and untainted creativity appealed as I considered all of the hopeful applicants and reviewed their credentials yet again. I understand the frustrations of every new graduate who receives rejections time after time since companies demand experience, and the old paradox surfaces that people need to be hired to get experience. I visualized the burned out look of long time job searchers and the feeling that their resumes get lost in deep black holes replacing Gail's optimistic mindset. I can practically touch the decision process as if it were happening right this moment.

Now, I am a businessman and I make decisions with my head, not with my heart, right? Just because she reminds me of my daughter does not mean I cannot choose experience and a proven record over a new graduate, despite her promising qualities.

Time for a coffee…I will buzz my secretary who makes an amazing brew exactly according to my tastes and never fails to stimulate my best thinking moments.

What are my primary goals here?
Getting Wings Publishing on the map
Identifying a unique brand and favor that people visualize when they think Wings
Hiring a dedicated, enthusiastic, talented staff whose strengths complement each other
Choosing people who are able to be open to new ideas and willing to experiment

It does appear that Gail fills these requirements better than the other applicants and will probably be eternally grateful that I gave her this exciting opportunity. Fostering unity and employee satisfaction also belongs on my priority list.

What a trip into the past. And that was a phenomenal stroke of genius, if I say so myself. Gail outdoes herself with her creative work. The positive feedback pings constantly in my inbox and translates into better sales and more authors wanting to utilize our services. Sometimes, I wonder if she realizes how much her talents have blossomed. She truly has the capacity to work in a top-notch company. Wait a minute, we are top-notch!

I know with complete certainty that Gail is beyond grateful to us for our training and allowing her to grow in her own unique way.

Funny, as I sit here musing, Gail is at my door. "Come in, Gail. What's wrong? You look a bit pale. You have been working hard. You know what? Take a few days paid vacation together with your husband. My favorite designer deserves a bonus for her golden handiwork.

"You want to talk with me. You have something to tell me. Gail, you are leaving our company! You are submitting notice with the required thirty-day notification and moving on. You will always be grateful.

"Well, I don't really know what to say. This comes as quite a shock and in my mind's eye, I pictured you as a fixture here at Wings for many years. Is there something you were unhappy with regarding your work situation? Is there any way you might be willing to reconsider? I cannot just simply accept this resignation without a proper conversation after all of these years of facilitating your rise to stardom. Please give me the courtesy of considering my request and go home, discuss this with your husband, and let's meet in three days. At that point, if this decision remains firm, I will have no choice but to accept this with a heavy heart. After all, Wings believes in employee satisfaction. Have a good afternoon Gail. I will see you on Thursday at 4:00."

A Piece of the Pie

JOY SPEAKS / DIANE SPEAKS:

Joy Speaks:

After a long day at work followed by an even longer evening of supper and homework, my feet were aching and my head was spinning, and I was dreaming fluffy dreams of collapsing in bed with a good book. Just then the phone rang; it was my friend, Diane. The last thing I wanted at that moment was a long phone call, but what could I do? Being kind isn't always convenient, and she seemed to really need to vent. So postponing my wistful dreams, I thrust my arms into a sink full of dishes, eyeing the clock nervously as the kids' bedtime ticked later and later. I listened, empathized, and um-hmed often enough to show my interest and concern.

"They really won't give Lisa her eighth grade diploma unless she brings up her math grade?" I was aghast. Lisa was such a sweet girl. What would become of her if she couldn't go to high school together with her friends and peers? And suddenly, just as I picked up the last dirty glass, epiphany struck.

"Diane!" I said, my voice brimming with excitement. "Why don't you send Lisa to me a few times a week? I can help her with her math!"

"Oh, Joy," Diane replied, and I could almost see her shaking wisps of auburn hair out of her green eyes. "I can't ask you for that kind of favor. I wasn't calling to ask you for practical help; I just needed your ear, that's all. I mean, you work full time, are juggling a family- how in the world would you have time for my daughter, too?"

"What are friends for?" I rejoined, setting the last sparkling glass in the drainer and breathing a sigh of relief. "I am a math teacher, after all, and I'd like to help. Send her to me a few times a week and she'll be up to snuff in no time; you'll see."

"Joy, you're a lifesaver," Diane breathed. "But as much as I don't want Lisa to be held back, I don't have money to pay you for tutoring a few times a week. I think the going rate is at least 50 dollars an hour, and there is just no way we can do that. I wish we could, but we're always tight, you know that. With a family, the needs are constant, and there never seems to be a month without some kind of major expense that sets us back yet again. People don't seem to eat out as much as they used to, either, so our pizza shop is struggling to stay afloat."

"Tell you what," I said, reaching for the broom and feeling very altruistic. "Talk with your husband and just pay me whatever you two think you can handle. Lisa needs to graduate, and that's all there is to it. This is the perfect solution."

"I don't know what to say," Diane replied. "You're amazing. I'll talk to George and get back to you."

We settled on ten dollars a session, and sometimes it was even less. But it didn't bother me. I watched Lisa grasp the concepts of pre-algebra that had been eluding her, and it was so rewarding. Her shy smile lit up her face when comprehension dawned, and I felt a deep bubble of satisfaction and accomplishment. She would graduate with her class where she belonged, and she would do so with confidence.

Our tutoring sessions continued for several months until finally Lisa felt comfortable swimming alone.

"I'm so glad," I told her as we said good-bye at our last session. "But if you ever have any questions, just call me- I'm happy to help."

A few weeks later, I had **A Day**. My phone rang very early in the morning- my very close friend was calling to tell me she had just been diagnosed with a malignancy, and we cried together. Then, on the way to school, I got rear-ended and wound up waiting an hour until a police officer showed up to assess the damage and make a report. So I was late to work, the kids were late to school, and I was in quite a state, feeling like I was playing the main part in a scene that I had not auditioned for. My students, perhaps sensing my tenuous state of mind, were climbing the walls, acting unusually restless and rowdy. I found myself wishing the clock hands would wind faster to bring this awful day to a close. As I drove home, I tried to breathe deeply and decided it was time for some self-care. There was simply no way I was in any condition to make supper, clean up from supper, and plunge into a typical, hectic, breathless evening. I'll get dinner from George's Chips, I decided, pleased with my decision. We rarely indulge in such luxuries, but today is anything but a regular day. Surely Diane and her husband would give us a discount, which would make it easier to handle this extra expenditure on our limited budget.

"Joy!" Diane greeted me warmly, cheeks flushed from working behind the counter. "What a nice surprise! What can I do for you?"

"Hi," I said. "Good to see you, too! I've had a really hard day, so I decided a treat was in order. How about two pies, two orders of spicy fries, and a family salad?" I asked. *I would love some soup and dessert, too. Should I? Or am I taking advantage? No, it's okay*, I told myself. *I gave her assistance when she was in need without a thought of reimbursement. For months. Now I'm the one in need. Life is a wheel- sometimes we give and sometimes we receive. And that's okay.*

"Um, can I add some of your famous onion soup and a dozen assorted cookies?"

"Of course." Diane was busily punching numbers into the register. "That'll be 75 dollars, please," Diane calculated, looking at me expectantly.

Huh? 75 dollars?! Where's my discount, or even my free supper? After I tutored Lisa for months, practically for free- is this my thanks? I don't get it!

Stymied, I fumbled for my credit card, while my emotions reached a hearty boil. *I would never have ordered the extras had I known she would charge me full price. But it's not just the money, it's the principle. Where is her gratitude? Maybe I should think twice before I offer my services the next time...*

Diane Speaks:

It is so hard to be on the receiving end. I feel so very needy. I remember when we use to play value games in high school and college, and I felt so righteous placing financial security on the bottom of my list. Financial security was just a value for materialistic people, not for the likes of me, a person thirsting for spiritual fulfillment. And yet, when my daughter needs a math tutor and I can't afford to pay appropriate value, I wonder: Is money only materialistic or will it help her to feel confident and master necessary skills? And when my children need new clothing or shoes and they feel deprived compared to most of their classmates, is that merely materialistic, or a healthy desire to live within the norms of their peer groups? Or yes, even when I just feel overwhelmed with the dual responsibilities of running our home and restaurant and cannot afford household help, which would ease the burden physically and emotionally, it seems to me that financial security is not merely a vehicle for materialistic pleasure.

And then we face these very difficult conflicts. I have a dear friend who also happens to be a math whiz who offered to tutor my daughter, Lisa, for almost nothing. She loves my Lisa, she loves teaching, and she does not need the money currently as her husband appears to be doing very well financially. She agreed to take a minimal token just to preserve my dignity. It is working beautifully- she has bonded so well with my Lisa, and I've watched how Lisa's confidence in math has soared. Prior to receiving this extra help, Lisa was convinced she had a math disability, that she was hopeless, and now she realizes she is capable of understanding. I can't even place a value on confidence and optimism, not to mention rescuing her from the ultimate humiliation of being held back if she hadn't been able to get past this hurdle.

I have been busily thinking of how to express this gratitude which transcends financial value. The easy way would be to invite her to a paid meal for her and her family in my restaurant. Yet, that almost seems tit for tat, not to mention that it may even offend her. She clearly wanted to help Lisa while being extremely sensitive to our precarious financial situation. To give her a meal and cut out our profit in some ways would undermine her efforts rather than honor them. It may be even more tricky if she happens to show up, which she does occasionally, to charge her the regular price. Yet, I know that at the end of the day, respecting a person's intentions and allowing them to give is also an act of giving. I have a different idea.

Every year, our school seeks a worthy couple to honor who truly personifies the attributes of kindness and generosity. I am calling the principal today and sharing my nomination. She deserves far more than a meal, which is eaten and digested. She deserves recognition so the community can emulate her ways. I bet we can even organize a surprise video with her children speaking about what it was like to grow up in her home.

It has been a long time since I have felt so excited by an idea. Additionally, it reminds me that money is one way to give, but here are other avenues that are perhaps even more meaningful.

You won't believe this, but here she comes now to purchase a meal. Was she eavesdropping on my thoughts? What a deserving honoree—always seeking ways to give while preserving the dignity of others. Although, every fiber in me wants to say "It's on the house," I will allow her to give in accordance to what she truly wants to do.

"Hi, Joy. What would you like to order today?"

Section Three: ICARE

OUTLINE OF INTERVENTIONS AND SAMPLE
INTERVIEWS FROM OUR STORIES

ICARE

INTERNAL COMPASSION AND
RELATIONSHIP ENHANCEMENT

There is no greater blessing than peaceful interpersonal relationships. Yet the challenges are genuine. We experience a wide range of emotional reactions in our interactions. Often, we wish that our anger would vanish together with the discomfort of any other negative emotions, as it does not make us feel very good about ourselves. Yet, suppression only backfires in the form of actual illness or potential inappropriate expression of our hurt or anger that just could not simply be wished away. We were not designed to be stones in a static state, but are meant to grow and change through our life experience.

How then can we achieve genuine peace?

Firstly, we need to recognize that the concept of not appeasing a person in the midst of anger applies to ourselves, too.

We learn to accept the sacred endeavor of working towards peace by first working through our emotions and owning them. It takes time to reach a calm and rational state where we can successfully navigate the turbulence, and forcing ourselves to do this prematurely will likely result in holding grudges or self-deception.

From a calm state, we are then ready to utilize emotionally intelligent power tools such as giving the benefit of the doubt and working to understand both our own and the other person's mindset. With understanding of the underlying concerns on both sides of a conflict, each side can look to determine what they might contribute to a win/win solution. They can prioritize formulating an action plan that is responsive to the key concerns of both sides involved in the disagreement.

The following questions are designed to take you through a path of honest reflection with the ultimate goal of achieving inner peace and using life experiences to refine character traits.

If you are in any type of abusive relationship, please seek help, as this questionnaire is designed for the normal aches and pains that we experience just by virtue of our human imperfection.

Not every question will apply to every situation. We will provide a few examples from our book where we utilized this method successfully to give you a taste of our recipe that can aid in working through our emotions. We would love to hear your feedback and your own creative additions that work for you.

These questions are a great starting point for enhanced self-awareness, which is essential to growth. If you would like to learn more about yourself, consider working with a relationship counselor. We wish you much joy and fulfillment while finding inner and interpersonal peace in your lives.

Assessment:

Take your temperature. On a scale of 1 – 10 where 10 is "I'm extremely agitated and upset" and 1 is "I'm cool as a cucumber," what number are you?

If your temperature registers as six or higher, this is not the time to discuss the situation with the other person.

It's not even time to force yourself to figure out the issue. Instead just allow yourself to feel what you are feeling and observe it, whatever it is, with acceptance. Ironically, change can only occur after we accept our current situation. Another way to understand this idea is to see this as a starting point in order to map out a path to your destination.

Take the time you need to cool down. There's a reason you are upset.

A deep breath can help, or a walk. How about splashing some cool water on your face, or having a soothing, refreshing drink? Be very kind to yourself while trying to make sense of the situation.

When your temperature has come down to five or lower, it's possible to do further work.

How?

Step 1: Acknowledge that something is bothering you or upsetting you. You are human, and as humans we have a wide range of emotions and responses. Every emotion can be channeled productively and effectively provide information to help us grow.

What is it? What specifically is upsetting?

What did the other person do that triggered your feelings? Be specific so we can understand this best together.

What impact did it have on you?

What might it remind you of from your past?

Sometimes, it is not the present event that is really upsetting us, but the episode triggered something painful from our past. Recognizing this fact can help us in the present.

What happened back then?

How is this similar?

The truth is that the only one you can change is yourself, no matter what is happening with the other person, no matter how disturbing their behaviors or apparent intentions may have been.

Step 2: With that in mind, how (if at all) might you have contributed to the situation and the other person's actions?

Step 3: What might your 'ideal self' want from you now?

Step 4: What do you need in order to move in the direction of your ideal self?

Step 5: How might you access the part of yourself that is compassionate and caring?

Step 6: How might you transcend your immediate need to be right about this and not feel the need to win and blame?

Step 7: Reflect on a time where you successfully navigated a conflict. How did that happen? What allowed you to reconnect? What (if anything) might you borrow from that experience?

Step 8: What would you advise someone you love who approached you with the same dilemma? Give yourself the gift of love and friendship and advise yourself accordingly.

Step 9: After the incident, ask yourself: Which part of this did I navigate well and how might I do better in the future?

Interventions from "What's the Big Deal" to help Beverly and Steve understand one another and repair their hurt.

Beverly: Oh my goodness. I'm so upset!

Self-Counselor: Take your temperature, what is it?

Beverly: Urgh. It's 11 on a scale of 1 – 10.

Self-Counselor: OK, let's take a walk.

Beverly: Sounds good. I do need to walk this anger off.

[Half an hour later]

Beverly: [taking a deep breath] OK, I think I can deal with this now.

Self-Counselor: Excellent! I am so proud of you for taking a little time for yourself and cooling down enough to think about it. So what specifically was upsetting?

Beverly: My husband couldn't empathize with me. I was in so much pain, so upset. I was reaching out to him for some support and I didn't get any. Just like always!

Self-Counselor: Oh, that sounds awful. What did your husband do to trigger those feelings?

Beverly: He said, "No big deal!" It's so dismissive, as if I'm a little girl and what I'm upset about is silly and unimportant.

Self-Counselor: And when you heard those words, what happened inside?

Beverly: They made me feel diminished, stupid, self-deprecating. I must be an awful person to be so upset over nothing. And I feel misunderstood by him.

Self-Counselor: It must feel horrible to think your own husband, the most important person in your life, doesn't understand you

Beverly: Exactly! Sometimes I wonder about our relationship, if we lack even that basic foundation.

Self-Counselor: I'm so glad you can admit your thoughts and feelings right now. I'm wondering if this is how you generally see him.

Beverly: I don't think so, but when he minimizes my pain, he seems harsh.

Self-Counselor: What might it remind you of from your past?

Beverly: My father always made light of anything I was upset about. His mouth would twitch, as if to stop a smile or laugh, and he'd say, "What are you so upset about, sweetie? This is small potatoes. Nothing should bother you like this. Don't cry. Forget about it." He always wanted me to be logical and less emotional. But I was just a little girl.

Self-Therapist: And?

Beverly: That made me think about what was bothering me even more, *and* I felt angry at myself because Daddy told me it was no big deal. So clearly there was something wrong with me. And I felt hurt on two levels with no one to talk to about it. Because Mommy would support Daddy to be sure I didn't see him in a bad light.

Self-Counselor: Wow! You must have felt confused and hurt while looking for someone who could help you make sense of your feelings

Beverly: I did! And, that's exactly how I feel now.

Self-Counselor: How did you get over it?

Beverly: Well, I guess I really didn't because that part of me easily flares when Steve says "No big deal."

Self-Counselor: Hmmmm. Well, how (in any way) might you have drawn the "No big deal" response from Steve?

Beverly: [indignantly] I DON'T THINK I DID. HE ALWAYS ACTS JUST LIKE DADDY!

Self-Counselor: Always?

Beverly: Well, when he doesn't want me to feel bad.

Self-Counselor: Oh, why doesn't he want you to feel bad?

Beverly: [angrily] HE HATES TO HEAR ME COMPLAIN AND EXAGGERATE.

Self-Counselor: [pauses and looks at her with compassion.]

Beverly: And, I guess if I think about it, he really feels awful when he thinks I'm in pain.

Self-Counselor: What tells you that?

Beverly: Well, if I allow myself to look at him at those times, I see sad eyes, as if he doesn't know what to do or say and just wants the discomfort to go away.

Self-Counselor: Uh huh.

Beverly: I think it's difficult for him to see me upset.

Self-Counselor: Why is that?

Beverly: Because he really does care and wants the best for me.

Self-Counselor: How can you help him be there for you at those times?

Beverly: I could prepare him. Part of the problem is that he wants to jump in and fix the situation for me, not realizing that

I just need him to listen. So, I might say, "Steve, could you please hear about my flailing upset for a minute, so I can get it out of my system? I know in the long run it's no big deal, but at the moment it's giving me heartache, even worse than my mother's cinnamon apple cake."

Self-Counselor: [Laughing], Worse than your mothers sickeningly sweet cake? Oh my goodness. That's got to be the worst discomfort. I remember that cake. Really lethal.

Beverly: [laughs]

Self-Counselor: What might happen if you asked him that?

Beverly: I think he would listen.

Self-Counselor: Wonderful. And, what do you think your ideal self wants?

Beverly: I think my ideal self wants two things. She wants me to be more confident in my own skin, and she wants me to have more of a sense of humor about what others say. Not to take it so seriously... And she wants me to communicate my needs to my husband honestly, understanding the good intention behind my husband's behavior. He really is a good man, you know. When I am not in this upset state, I recognize that.

Self-Counselor: In what ways is he really a good man?

Beverly: He works very hard for the family, he's sweet and loving most of the time, he gives a lot of time and attention to our children, he encourages me to take time for myself, to do the activities I enjoy, to take time with my friends, and he really wants to be there for me- no matter what. I just need to tell him more clearly how he could best support me.

Self-Counselor: Sounds like a wonderful plan.

Beverly: Thank you. I can breathe again. I think I'll go make a nice dessert for Steve. One that won't give him heartburn.

They both laugh.

∴

Steve: I just don't know what to do with Beverly. She gets so rattled when someone says anything to her that she doesn't want to hear.

Self-Counselor: That sounds like a difficult situation for you.

Steve: It is! And then, when I try to help, she attacks me with a laundry list of how I disappoint her.

Self-Counselor: That can't be much fun, to say the least.

Steve: Fun? Who can have any fun when your wife is so angry with you?

Self-Counselor: True, it colors everything in life and clearly impacts you deeply.

Steve: It sure does. It makes me feel like all my efforts to please her don't even register. They're worthless. I'm worthless. And I just want to get as far away as possible to avoid getting any more assaults on my character.

Self-Counselor: You want to escape from the pain and the feeling of not getting it right with her. Do you recall ever feeling this way before?

Steve: My mother, whom I adored, would get so upset at the littlest things that others said, and it would make me feel powerless to help. I just couldn't please her no matter how I tried. I would offer something, and she'd just get angrier at me, as if I got in the way of her need to let her feelings out about something else, and then I became the focus of her disturbance. It was very scary. I wanted to help and I just added fuel to the fire.

Self-Counselor: So what do did you do?

Steve: I'd run to my room and play video games until I heard her puttering around in the kitchen and singing. That would be my signal that reentry was safe, and she was back to her normal, loving self.

Self-Counselor: That sounded like a good coping mechanism on your part. And you even used the time to cool off. What a smart thing to do. And now, knowing what you know about your wonderful wife and mother and their sensitivity to how others see them, what might you have done differently?

Steve: I have to remember that even though a friend's comment might seem silly, exaggerated or unimportant from my perspective, to my sweet wife it could be devastating. I just don't want her to hurt. Especially over such nonsense. I think she's absolutely beautiful and always will be in my eyes.

Self-Counselor: What a wonderful thought about your wife. You are both so lucky to have each other. How can you move forward?

Steve: I think it's a good idea to step out of my past, to see that this is my dear wife who needs me and my job is to just listen compassionately for a little while. She never asks for a lot. She just needs me to be present and reflect her feelings. I don't have to be the big man and fix everything. Listening tenderly is enough.

Self-Counselor: That sounds perfect! What a caring husband. Let me know how it goes.

Marla works through her anger with her own inner Self-Counselor.

Marla: I'm fuming. So glad Mom is leaving today. I just don't think I could take it anymore!

Self-Counselor: You sound very angry and upset.

Marla: That's an understatement! Every time she comes, I go out of my way to make her comfortable, be respectful, and yet all I get is a barrage of criticism about how I ruined her son's life and hers. I hate to say it, but I feel like I have been a victim of verbal and emotional abuse.

Self-Counselor: That sounds very painful. You wish she would value your efforts and see the happy family you have with her son. Instead, she just seems to get stuck in "if only" land.

Marla: Exactly. Am I really so bad? [Heavy tears]

Self-Counselor: Absolutely not. She's really tough to please, and I feel for you.

Marla: Really? I appreciate that.

Self-Counselor: Well, yeah. You said it yourself. Her words are abusive even if that is not her intention. That's hard for anyone to deal with, don't you think?

Marla: It has been very hard and frustrating. I want to love her and have a close connection, yet somehow I always end up feeling that I am a disappointment to her...and that hurts. And then, there's the value around money that seems to be at the root of a lot of the friction. We don't have the money for all the things I wish we could give the children, but I really don't care about fancy clothes and jewelry like she does. I mean, it certainly would be easier if Sol made a more lucrative income.

We have been blessed with a large family, and there are so many expenses. But he truly loves his work and is so good at it, and the students are growing and value his guidance. And even more importantly, our children look up to their father and love him dearly.

Self-Counselor: It sounds like you are generally happy with the way your family life is going but your mother-in-law touches a nerve- otherwise, why this would be so upsetting?

Marla: I guess there is a part of me that resents the struggle and wishes we didn't have to count our pennies so carefully. And, most of the time I am happy, yet somehow when she speaks about finances, it brings up my own feelings of worry and uncertainty. Somehow I want to prove to her that the true wealth lies in an upright life and I wish she would see it when she looks at us. When she appears to find fault, I feel inadequate, as if I am not doing a good enough job demonstrating the beauty of our living according to higher values. If she equates our lifestyle with deprivation on my account, I have failed miserably.

Self-Counselor: That's a lot. It sounds like part of you wishes you could have more money and the other part is very grateful for the gifts you have and the choices you have made. And you feel this strong pressure to prove to your mother in law that you are all thriving. What's the worst part for you, assuming that all of these feelings are grounded in truth?

Marla: I feel shame that we may not have enough to take care of them or that we'll have to sacrifice our family's needs to provide for them as they begin to age. I also feel guilty that I find it hard to love my mother-in-law unconditionally. She's such a thorn in my self-esteem.

Self-Counselor: It's a tough one. It is hard to love someone who's so critical, especially in an area where you feel so vulnerable.

Marla: But she's still my husband's mother. Her blood is carried in my children. And it's normal for her to fear aging and becoming dependent. Who can she count on if not us?

Self-Counselor: That's very generous and compassionate of you, dear Marla.

Marla: Thank you.

Self-Counselor: How can I help you feel more generous and compassionate towards yourself?

Marla: Well, the affirmation you just gave me was a good start. I need to know that my mother-in-law's assessment of me is not who I am, nor does it define me. I need to endorse myself for supporting Sol in choosing his own path and pursuing his dreams.

Self-Counselor: Mmhmmm.... And?

Marla: I want to remind myself that underneath my mother-in-law's quills pulses a heart full of fear for the wellbeing of her family and trepidations for her own future. So I have to stop allowing it to trigger me and send me into a frenzy of self-recrimination. It's really hers and not mine. **And** I'm not going to change her. The only one I have any control over is myself.

Self-Counselor: That's pretty impressive work you just did. It truly is. I'm so honored to be a part of your journey of self-acceptance and realization.

Marla: Thank you. I can breathe again. Believe it or not, there is even a small voice, a whisper, that wants her to come again before too long, so I can try not to be triggered in the same way after coming to this realization.

Self-Counselor: Wow! Marla, I really respect the person you are and who you are striving to be.

April utilizes the ICARE Model after being fired as she works as her own "self-counselor".

April's self: I can't believe my boss fired me. Me? After all I've done for them? Are they kidding? I thought I was getting a raise and now this?! I just can't reconcile this. How could they?! This is so totally devastating!

Self-Counselor: Sounds awful...

April: It *is* awful. What am I missing? Did I do something wrong? I revamped their systems, made everything run more smoothly and efficiently- is this how they repay good work? I'm just so terribly upset.

Self-Counselor: Makes perfect sense that this would be upsetting. Who wouldn't be after all that effort? What's the worst part?

April: It makes me doubt myself. As much as I'm upset with them, I wonder if I did something wrong so I blame myself, and my self-esteem, which was pretty high while I was working, just took a nose dive. I feel so unappreciated and at the same time I question my worth.

Self-Counselor: I'm so sorry. Sounds very sad and hurtful. What might this remind you of from your past?

April: I hadn't even thought of the past, but now that you mention it- it reminds me of a time when I was twelve and the choir leader chose my friend for a solo instead of me. I really thought I had better pitch and more expression. Her decision shocked me, just like what happened now. And, the same words want to scream out of my throat: "It's not fair!" It truly feels just as unfair as when I was a young child.

Self-Counselor: Very interesting! How are these two situations similar?

Self: Well, the similarities are quite strong because in both situations I did a job that I really believed was worthy of commendation. But, instead of being valued, they let me go; I was dispensable. What person would want to feel like a paper towel tossed out once it's fulfilled its purpose?

Self-Counselor: [shaking her head back and forth in commiseration and silently asking me to continue]

April: Being rejected hurts so badly, especially when I truly feel qualified and capable. It would still hurt if that were not the case, but at least on some level, it would make sense. And the idea of telling my husband that I no longer have a job seems so humiliating. It sets off my anger all over again when I think about the ramifications of this loss. Couldn't they have creatively designed a way to keep me on board if they truly valued what I brought to the table?

Self-Counselor: It's not just the fact that they laid you off, but the implications of it as well?

April: Exactly! Adjustment to a new reality takes time as it definitely came as a shock. And it makes me see how much my identity is tied up with my employment status. Ugh. Do I need other people to tell me that I have talents in order to feel good about myself? So hard to realize that there is still part of me that craves the gold stars.

Self-Counselor: It takes a lot of courage and honesty to look at yourself so openly. Very impressive!

April: Thank you. I guess I need to stay with these thoughts and feelings for a little while and try to understand why this is so significant for me.

Self-Counselor: Yes! If you let yourself feel your feelings and think about the current situation and how it ties back to other events in your life, you'll be able to understand and come to terms with it.

April: Right, because if I give myself permission to feel my feelings and then think about it from the perspective of the bigger picture, I will be able to move beyond it in a healthier way – I want to learn from this experience. And you know, when one door closes, another opens. I trust that everything that occurs is designed to help me grow and will ultimately be for my benefit, even if it is hard to perceive in the moment.

Self-Counselor: Excellent! You're already doing this work right here and now! It must feel deeply satisfying.

April: It really does. I want to get back on track, moving towards my ideal self.

Self-Counselor: Your ideal self? Who is she? How is she different from the self that is here and now?

April: She's more logical, reasonable, calm and able to handle challenges without losing her sense of self-respect.

Self-Counselor: How can we encourage that part of yourself?

April: I can open myself up and be vulnerable, which will invite warmth and encouragement from my loving family and friends. They really are very supportive and will not judge me as I do.

Self-Counselor: Excellent! Wow. I can tell from your calmer demeanor and slower heart rate that you're already beginning to feel better. I'm so happy for you and proud of you, my dear little self.

April: [blushing shyly] Thank you.

Self-Counselor: [beams an illuminated smile at me, encouraging me to continue.]

April: [Animated] In addition, I can accept that offer from my boss of writing a sincere letter of recommendation.

Self-Counselor: [nods in agreement.]

April: And you know what? I really need to remind myself that any particular job does not define my identity. I am the same person today as I was yesterday while sitting at that desk, except perhaps more sensitive and compassionate towards people who may have gone through similar challenges.

Self-Counselor: Excellent!

April: I'm reflecting on how I can grow from this challenge. It's so interesting that in acknowledging my hurt feelings instead of pretending they don't exist, in thinking it through with you, the pain subsides and I find myself experiencing more self-acceptance and a place of inner serenity.

Self-Counselor: That's heartwarming and incredibly insightful.

Betty uses the ICARE model to work through her hurt at being criticized for misallocating charity funds.

Self-Counselor: You seem upset, what's going on?

Betty's Self: I tried to do something good and instead I got yelled at.

Self-Counselor: That must hurt.

Betty: It really did and made me angry. It felt unjust.

Self-Counselor: So what happened? What did she do that was so upsetting?

Betty: She accused me of not following the protocol and trying to be pushy about how the money should be allocated.

Self-Counselor: And...

Betty: I didn't know that I couldn't earmark funds. I had no idea that I was stepping on her toes. I just wanted to help Sally. That poor lady is really struggling and suddenly her rent is due! Her pain was intense. How could I just sit there and not do something for her? I knew there was something I could do. My intentions were pure.

Self-Counselor: So what did Rhoda do that was so upsetting?

Betty: She made it sound like I was purposely going behind her back, like I was sneaking. I almost felt like a naughty child getting caught red-handed.

Self-Counselor: Uh huh- it sounds like you feel a need to defend yourself.

Betty: That's exactly right. She was condescending. Like I should have known. It was so blatantly clear, but it wasn't. I had done similar fundraising before, and my manner of handling it was perfectly accepted and actually appreciated. I just wanted to help. And I thought of Rhoda as someone I respected, someone who was such a kind person. I thought she would be delighted. Instead, she felt put upon and overlooked. Ugh. Exactly opposite of what I expected to happen.

Self-Counselor: What might this remind you of from the past?

Betty: I'm thinking...When something I thought was for the good backfired...Hmmmmm. What comes to mind is doing my sister's chores and getting in trouble with my mother, because Mommy wanted her to do her own chores.

Self-Counselor: Good! Tell me more. What did that feel like?

Betty: I knew my sister hated to clean and I really enjoyed it. So when I told her I'd take care of her work so she could go spend time with her friends, I thought I was doing something good. Instead, my mother got angry at me and my sister. I felt sad, disappointed and confused, wondering how a good deed could back fire like that. And even guilty that I got my sister in trouble when I was just trying to help.

Self-Counselor: How did your mother express her upset?

Betty: It wasn't only what she said but the way she said it. She made me feel guilty, like I was doing something sneaky and underhanded rather than praising me for my extra work that would allow my sister to have joy. Shouldn't I have gotten some positive reinforcement for my selflessness?

Self-Counselor: It was very kind of you to want your sister to enjoy herself and your mother's response must have been painful. Do you think, perhaps your mother was trying to protect you and your sister at the same time?

Betty: Well, it didn't feel like it at the time, but I do tend to overextend myself and then get exhausted or cranky and can feel underappreciated for all I do. And perhaps she wanted my sister to accept her responsibilities rather than avoid them.

Self-Counselor: That makes sense.

Betty: I understand in retrospect that perhaps I should have found out about the guidelines around distributing charity. I thought what I was doing was fair and just, but I can see that even though I found the money for Sally, it was perhaps not my place to tell the agency how to distribute it. I didn't know. I just didn't know.

Self-Counselor: Wow. That acknowledgment took a lot of courage, self-reflection, and honesty. I don't know how many people could be that honest with themselves.

Betty: Thank you. [Deep breath] It's not easy to take a close look at yourself when you're enveloped in a halo.

Self-Counselor: That's the hardest time to try to grow, when you feel you've done something out of all good intentions. Makes total sense to me that you would feel unappreciated and misunderstood under the circumstances.

Betty: I need to breathe and realize that in the crisis of someone's need, perhaps I could pause and reflect on possibilities. I could have found out more about how this fund works instead of forging ahead like a knight in shining armor. When I think about it now, it would make sense that Rhoda could have felt insulted or belittled in my trying to be the savior when she was adhering to the rules. Maybe I hurt her feelings while I was being self-righteous about my actions.

Self-Counselor: You are amazing! What an incredible insight. Look how far you've journeyed from your initial reactions of anger and hurt to having compassion for Rhoda. That's truly extraordinary. I'm in awe.

Betty: [Blushes and murmurs] Thank-you. I loved my sister so much and she hated housework. She was much more extraverted and blossomed in her interactions with others. And she always made a difference with them. But I'm a homebody and I love doing things that make our home a little nicer. I just didn't understand why Mommy wanted us to do the same work. It was so satisfying to me to see my sister happy, so why couldn't I do more of the housework while she did community service? It seemed like a fair trade to me. Especially when she came home glowing and I could benefit from her light spirit. Now, years later, I've tried to emulate her and be more like her. When I reached out to the benefactors, I felt like her wonderful way of contacting people and inviting their collaboration was inside of me. I learned that from her. It was a blessing.

Self-Counselor: And nothing that happened here takes any of that away from you.

Betty: That's true, but if I truly want to do this good deed in a complete way, I think I'll go apologize to Rhoda. I would much rather do an act of charity without causing rough edges.

Self-Counselor: That's sounds like a wonderful idea for a growing person like you.

Karla successfully works through her fear of sharing her illness with Steve using the ICARE model.

Karla's Self: I'm so frightened that Steve is going to reject me for my health issues.

Self-Counselor: It is scary to reveal yourself and be vulnerable when you like him and see him as a possible life partner.

Karla: It really is! How will I feel if he no longer wants me? And if he walks away, will I ever find anyone else? Will I ever be able to get married? [Tears forming]

Self-Counselor: [softly] You really are terrifying yourself about this, aren't you?

Karla: Well how else can I feel? It really is terrifying. I don't want to tell him. And what could be more important than finding the right marriage partner? And [voice trembling as fear mounts again] if I don't reveal the truth, what kind of partnership would that be? I can't live a lie.

Self-Counselor: That is for sure. You want a relationship built on trust. Do you think that there is more going on inside of you than meets the eye? What might this remind you of from your past? When else have you been frightened like this about the possibility of being rejected?

Karla: That's just it. Never. I lived a charmed life. I was loved by my friends, cherished by my family. I excelled in school and was respected by my teachers. It was almost as if I had the magic touch. Everything was so easy and so rewarding. Until that awful diagnosis.

Self-Counselor: Awful?

Karla: Yes. Now I might not be good enough. I'm no longer perfect. I'm damaged goods now.

Self-Counselor: Maybe it's a blessing in disguise.

Karla: What do you mean? How could this be any kind of blessing?

Self-Counselor: Well, what do you think?

Karla: Hmm... you may be right. It's teaching me humility and not to take my blessings for granted. I appreciate my health more than I ever did. I have more compassion for others when they're struggling. I think I might not have been so accepting before. I think it will probably make me a better mother who will be able to empathize with my babies when they're unhappy.

Self-Counselor: And that's a damaged person?

Karla: Well, maybe not so bad.

Self-Counselor: So even if this particular man is not the right one, someone with such caring traits and other stellar qualities has to be a wonderful prospect for the right man.

Karla: Do you think the right man will see me beyond my illness?

Self-Counselor: You are far more than this problem that you're suffering- it does not define you. It's just a condition that comes and goes. I believe you will resolve it for the best.

Karla: Thank you for believing in me! I'm going to face my fear and tell Steve. I know it will be all right, no matter what the result will be.

Dear Readers,

We hope you have enjoyed relating to the characters in this book as much as we did. The more we put ourselves in their shoes, the closer and more compassionate we felt towards them. As we observe, we learn. As our defenses go down when we look at others, our openness to self-awareness is heightened. Allow us to respond to a couple of frequently asked questions.

When do I work on solving these issues with my own self as therapist and when do I seek professional help?

If the issue continues to torment you and interfere with the quality of life and your attention to your family and responsibilities, it is time to seek professional assistance. Asking for help demonstrates courage and a deep desire to grow. Sometimes, we all need an objective listener to help us uncover the obstacles that prevent us from moving forward.

If there is any danger of abuse or emotional manipulation, please seek help immediately.

I thought negative emotions like anger and jealousy are wrong. Why should I acknowledge them?

To rid ourselves of negative emotions that we experience, the first step is to acknowledge that the feeling exists. Without that first step, bad feelings fester, hurting us and eventually other people as well. The second step is recognizing with compassion what makes sense about the feeling and about the challenging situation that triggered it.   Thirdly, we can ask ourselves, what do I and others want in this situation? And last, what might be a better way to get that desire satisfied?

To rid ourselves of unwanted anger, for example, we can start by noticing our anger.

Look at what triggered it.

With this knowledge, looking at what we ourselves want in that triggering situation can launch new thoughts about how to more successfully get what we want.

Adding understanding about the concerns of others in the problem situation will soften our anger with compassion, and also enable us to find mutually agreeable solutions.

Moving forward this way, the anger diminishes

Were we looking through your window when we wrote our book?

This is probably the most common reaction, demonstrating the normalcy of human emotional responses and the struggles that we all share in terms of working on our character traits.

The answer is no.

May God help you actualize your potential and derive tremendous pleasure from all of your relationships.

—Mrs. Ellen Gendelman MS, LPC, CPC

—Mrs. Renee Jaspan

About the Author

Ellen Gendelman MS, LPC, CPC is a licensed psychotherapist and certified professional coach who specializes in working with relationships. She cherishes her own roles as wife, mother and grandmother. A veteran educator, and motivational speaker, she has a passion for helping people grow and maximize their potential. She can be contacted by phone at 248-915-9122 or at awindowwithin@gmail.com for speaking engagements, consultations or counseling appointments in person or remotely. She welcomes your visits to her website at www.awindowwithin.net

www.ingramcontent.com/pod-product-compliance
Lightning Source LLC
Chambersburg PA
CBHW031414290426
44110CB00011B/374